CARMELITE MONASTERY
W9-ABR-922

CONFESSION

CONFESSION

The Encounter with Christ in Penance

ADRIENNE VON SPEYR

HERDER AND HERDER

HERDER AND HERDER NEW YORK
232 Madison Avenue, New York 16, N. Y.

Original edition "Die Beichte", Johannes Verlag, Einsiedeln.
Translated by A. V. Littledale

1st Edition 1964
2nd Impression 1964
3rd Impression 1965

Nihil Obstat: Ioannes M. T. Borton. S. T. D., L. S. S. Censor deputatus
Imprimatur: † Georgius L. Craven, Epus. Sebastopolis, Vic. Gen.
Westmonasterii, die 17 Martii 1964

The Nihil Obstat and Imprimatur are a declaration that a book or pamphlet
is considered to be free from doctrinal or moral error.
It is not implied that those who have granted the Nihil Obstat and Imprimatur
agree with the contents, opinions or statements expressed.

234.166

Library of Congress Catalog Card Number: 64-15376
First published in West Germany © 1964 Herder KG
Printed in West Germany by Herder

CONTENTS

PREFACE

Adrienne von Speyr's book on Confession clearly occupies a central place in her work. The great commentary on St. John in particular, the books on prayer, on Our Lady, on the Passion according to St. Matthew,[1] in fact all her books, revolve round the act and the attitude of confession, the personal and sacramental encounter between sinner and God, the perfect openness of which is the condition of grace, vocation and prayer.

The new element in the author's view of confession, fully brought out in the present book, is its basis in the doctrine of the Trinity and, in particular, in that concerning Christ. The Cross (which comprises the whole doctrine of the Incarnation) is the archetype of confession; and, therefore, sacramental confession is, in a very strict sense, a following of Christ. The present work brings out very fully the vast implications of this doctrinal conception. It does not set out a completed system so much as provide a wealth of ideas and suggestions which both theologian and layman will find deep satisfaction in pursuing further.

[1] *The Word* and *Meditations on the Gospel of St. John* have appeared in English, published by William Collins & Sons and Harvill Press, London 1953 and 1959 resp.

The treatment from a trinitarian and christological standpoint necessarily entails a comprehensive view of the ecclesial aspect of the sacrament. Here the author is in line with the modern dogmatic and historical approach, but her own basic conceptions permit her to add much that is both original and valuable. How rightly her initial emphasis is placed is shown in her short final chapter on what is a *crux theologorum,* the confession of saints, which, seen in the light of her exposition, offers no further difficulty. I have already indicated elsewhere that the relation of the saints to confession, the manifold effect it has within the Church, has been specially treated in a book by the author as yet unpublished. The relation between baptism and confession will also be dealt with in a later work.

The present work is also characterized by being both speculatively profound and practically simple. Its practical character, the application to the individual confession, is clear on every page.

It is becoming customary now to speak of the sacrament of penance rather than of confession. This may be justified in a superficial, historical view, inasmuch as confession, in the early centuries, was seen predominantly in its penitential aspect. Then, however, the sacrament was in its infancy; and, since now, in its mature form, this aspect is by no means central, and barely enters into the dogmatic exposition, we see no reason to forego the name, confession, a word which indicates its principal element.

Hans Urs von Balthasar

1. INTRODUCTION: THE IMPULSE TOWARDS CONFESSION

WHENEVER we find ourselves in some critical situation involving freedom of choice, we look for a solution or a way out, sometimes, also for a basic principle – though a way out is what we prefer. Man is out to improve his position, to achieve a more satisfying existence, greater success; and only when his life falls short of his desire does he look for the cause of his failure. Then in the course of his search he is forced to consider the state of his own life. He tries to understand his position, to justify it, and so, perhaps, is led to acknowledge that circumstances are stronger than he, that he is powerless to change his condition, because he has to meet forces more potent than his. Yet, at the very moment he concludes that he is not to be blamed, he often finds himself in a deep disquiet and the suspicion of some hidden guilt.

Most people are incapable of analysing their own way of life. They need to discuss it with another and look for someone, not so much to hear his views as to have the chance of expressing exactly what troubles them; more especially, perhaps, to strengthen their own opinion by the reasons they adduce. Though what is said may not alter the situation, relief is gained from seeing it clearly and recognizing it to be ineluctable.

There are many for whom that kind of heart-to-heart talk is so much of a saving anchor, that once it is over, they sink back into a certain hopelessness. The discussion was their last hope; its failure proves that there is nothing more to be done, and they become more tepid than before, inert and "resigned".

Often enough these discussions are arranged so that they are bound to be ineffectual and the result a foregone conclusion. The person in question, though alleging his will to change his disposition in some way, fundamentally wills no alteration whatever. He choses his partner so that no effective intervention is possible. The partner's function is simply to nod assent. He makes a careful selection of the matter he confides, and the sketch he presents does not correspond with reality. Then, of course, any discussion remains fruitless. There are always people who, after talking with, say, a neighbour or someone on a like footing, suddenly betake themselves to what they conceive to be a higher plane, for example, to their doctor. The doctor's consulting-room is, indeed, where most such discussions are held. But what the doctor is told is usually only one aspect of the matter, because very few people are willing to listen to uncongenial advice. Almost everyone wants confirmation of his view, and is prepared to change only in matters of no moment. Often enough, they only want to use the doctor's opinion as a weapon against a third party, so as to change someone else's conduct rather than their own.

Most people indulge in self-justification. They like nothing better than to be told: "Your daughter ought really to see that . . .", "It is high time your husband . . .". They gratefully accept any new weapon for their battle with their environment. But their situation is unchangeable; their life is subject to ineluctable necessity. A wife is not happy with her husband, because by the evening she is too tired. She does not like going with him to the cinema, because her sight is bad. The same with people's faults; these are unavoidable, because, in any case, they do the best they can. They seem to be standing on a precarious scaffold; if anyone were to shake it, they would be hurled to their death. "My nerves will not stand another talk with my husband . . .". Their estimates of their environment are bound to be mistaken, because they have never taken the trouble to understand the life of other people and to share it with them in love. Yet people like that feel the urge to tell others how badly off they are, what an exacting and arduous life they lead; they want sympathy and at the same time to be supported in their negative attitude to others. No doubt they need to talk things over, but they lay down the rules for discussion. And, acknowledging no rules but their own, they feel perfectly free to express their own views without admitting objections. Most discussions are, therefore, mere gossiping about oneself and one's imagined condition. So the discussion often starts on the wrong lines, and many fall into the hands of irresponsible, unfitted and unscrupulous people. It may result in some sort of alleviation, but not in a real change.

If one were to describe real confession to such persons, the preparation and the insight required, they would either see it only as a derivative of what they call discussion, or else be terrified at the prospect of seeing themselves at last as they really are. For it would mean bringing their whole life under a principle which might well entail stringent, unforeseeable demands upon them. What they call discussion never goes below the surface. Even if the need of which they speak is deeply felt, it is treated in a superficial way. Consequently, it is never thoroughly examined, either as to its origin or its content. Their solitariness is a function of their inability to engage in a real heart to heart talk.

Anyone who, in virtue of his calling, deals with other people's problems, and gives the impression of personal concern, can thus easily build up a clientele. He may simply possess the art of listening attentively, and so arouse confidence, with the result that all sorts of people come and tell him the most unlikely things. They draw consolation and profit from the mere fact of the time devoted to them. They feel happy at being received and allowed to talk about themselves. In addition, there are various methods and techniques, as that of psycho-analysis, which try to bring help and relief by probing into a person's present state, and, from the resonances confidently expected, build up an image of the whole man. They bring into the open the emotional drives, the erotic impulses in their most or least conscious manifestations, using them to explain a man's whole conduct, to attribute to him a significance wholly deriving from his instincts, and leaving him with the feeling of being properly understood at last. And since a course of treatment lasts a long time, the patient feels himself uplifted, and, if the period coincides with his acute difficulties, he will afterwards be of the opinion that it helped him positively and permanently. Those sent away cured are often people who have been given *some* explanation of the most primitive things, such that, in all their conflicts, they can always hold on to it, while they remain blind to all that does not fit into the scheme. Instead of gaining access, through discussion, to the richness and variety of the real world, they are cut off from it, since all that does not fall in with the established method of analysis is explained away. Yet not every method needs to be as narrow as psycho-analysis. There are many ways by which it is thought possible to help people. They can be brought to a more social attitude and so discover hitherto concealed aspects of existence. All these methods, however, are human methods, formulae someone has devised to be applied, rigidly or loosely, to a number of cases. And being human in origin, they necessarily take account of only a restricted side of the personality. This even applies to a method which makes use of expressly religious means, such as prayer.

For, in the last resort, it is only the soul's creator who can treat it in such wise that it becomes what he intends it to be. He alone can heal it, by means he alone knows and makes available and ordains for the purpose. All other relationships between counsellors and counselled are based upon a need. God's way, however, which is confession, is founded on obedience, obedience to God on the part both of the counsellor and the counselled. Man may, certainly, feel a need for confession, but his confession is real only when made in obedience to God. The confessor hears the sins of his penitent exclusively out of obedience to God, not on the ground of any need. God has himself appointed the place where he wills the sinner to be treated; that place is the cross, and the confessional set up under its shadow. To follow the way God prescribes is a fundamental act of obedience to him, the way he indicates as the only right way, the only one which brings healing.

This does not mean that discussion of one's spiritual concerns, outside confession and ecclesiastical authority, is useless or harmful. But when it is initiated and conducted in the right spirit, it leads, sooner or later, directly or indirectly, to the act of confession. As for matters of lesser consequence, they can well be dealt with by methods less searching than confession.

Once a man realizes, in however elementary fashion, that he stands before God, once he knows that, like Adam, he was made by God, that he has been redeemed by Christ, who, by his death, has opened to him access to the Father and the gates of heaven, then he will, by a kind of necessity, expect such a thing as confession, conscious, as he is, of being a sinner, and placed between the two poles of birth and death. He will expect God to make it possible for him to turn, at any moment, to a centre that God himself indicates and makes accessible. Every man has some sort of feeling that "he cannot go on like this any more". This leads him to inquire into possible alternative courses, and, perhaps, how, from God's point of view, he ought to continue; how God has envisaged his life, not only in its totality, but from the present point of time onwards; if God awaits something definite that he can and must discharge in God's own way. Perhaps he feels, considering his own freedom or others who live in a like state of freedom, unable to come up to this expectation of God's, that it is not enough to declare his condition according to his own or another's formula and shift the burden on to the other, in order to set himself anew on the right way, making his life from birth and death a unity. Whatever he can do in the way of declaring himself, apart from confession, may afford him some temporary relief; but he knows that the period of alleviation is merely one among many disconnected sections of his life, and that what really matters is to bring them all together into a single whole.

Suppose you are a friend of mine, and that I say to you: "I can't carry on any more." We talk over the situation together; perhaps we discover where I took the wrong turning, we go back to my infancy. The insight gained will help me to start afresh. But in discussions like this the individual is always looked at in isolation rather than as one of a community composed of saints and sinners. The laws, however, of the community of saints and sinners can only be known to God. In confession, it is true, I am this individual sinner, but I am, at the same time, a member of humanity, a fallen member. Thus, the person is seen quite differently in confession and in analysis.

In the former, he is viewed both as an individual and as a social being; he is seen in his totality, in a view that comprises the world as a whole, God's relation to it, the first and last things – even if this whole framework is only glimpsed momentarily, or felt in an indirect manner. Since, then, the situation is quite a different one, the remedy is different. For it is the truth of God that is at work, not the truth of man, not even the truth of his soul, of his being, his deepest self, but, quite simply, the truth of God. None of the human methods seriously considers this divine truth. At best, they reserve it for when death comes, and are of no help in bringing man to the state he will have to be at death.

As long as it is man who brings help to man, and all is on the human level, only human means can be applied. Everything that supervenes on this level can only be considered accidental, external, with a positive or negative significance, but there is no question of the unity of the internal and external. Sessions with an analyst can only provide me with "maxims of conduct", valid for the present, but to be replaced by others when the situation changes. Confession, on the contrary, confronts man with his divine destiny, setting him in that final and definitive context.

Until he goes to confession, a person feels himself free to speak or be silent, as he wills. What he hates about confession is not the humiliation of what is disclosed, of being shown to be a sinner – he knew that, to some degree, already –, but the fact that he must capitulate utterly in confessing everything; he is deprived of all freedom of choice, except that between manifesting everything or nothing. In his totality he is sick, and must be healed. That is the first humiliation. The second is that he is but one of many, and has to observe the same formalities as all the rest, including such externals as confessing at the time prescribed. All are treated alike, all placed on the same footing. At the very moment when one is confessing the most personal things, one is left without choice, like any other sinner, just one of the queue. There is absolutely no question of my special "case" and all that seemed to make it so interesting to me, and that I loved to expatiate upon to my audience. Confession is, above all, acknowledgement; not only of my sins, but of God and his precepts, even of the Church with its weakness and its many questionable and repellent aspects.

I can talk over my life with someone else without incurring any obligation. I may feel gratitude to him for listening to me or feel that I have been a bother to him, but I remain free to retire again within myself. Confession, however, is not the same, not just a single act. No aspect can be taken in isolation; the act of confession expressly concerns the whole man, his whole life and outlook, his whole relation to God.

If I tell a third person that I am discussing my life with someone, he will, as a rule, say he is glad I have found someone to help me. Somehow or other, he will think more highly of me. But if I tell him I go to confession and that it has a redeeming power for me, I shall go down in his estimation — those who do not go to confession nearly always object to it. It impinges on man's freedom, affronts his self-righteousness; it is unmodern, 'medieval' in fact, bound up, as it is, with so many externals. Those who do not confess feel superior; and, by confessing, I put myself among the "lower orders". On the other hand everyone acknowledges the value of human advice and use it or not as he sees fit, attends to it as far as suits them. There is no "suiting oneself" in the confessional.

Those who want advice, impelled by some inner necessity, should continue until they are able to face this necessity squarely, until they can see into the motives driving them, and, for a short time at least, have so far emerged from the situation they thought inescapable that their own guilt stands out clearly; at any rate, till it occurs to them there might be a simple connection between the situation and their guilt. For, in the majority of cases, even when a person knows and admits he has often done wrong and continues to do so, he still regards himself as a fixed entity which is not really affected by his sins. It is only when he comes to face his sins that he discovers the connection, which is far more than a mere parallelism between "destiny" and "personal inadequacy", as most people imagine it to be. They see, on the one hand, their thwarted state, their burdensome fate, and, on the other, themselves, admittedly with some shortcomings. But we come to see the unity of the two only when God himself holds up the mirror before us, provided that we have the courage to look in it.

This mirror is God's Incarnate Son, who became like us in all things, sin excepted. And so, whoever wants to learn how to confess must first look at the life of the Son of God. There he will learn what confession is, how it was intended, and how it works.

2. CONFESSION IN THE LIFE OF CHRIST

Foundation in the Trinity

GOD stands before God in the attitude that befits God. This can be considered analogous to confession, since it is the attitude in which God shows himself as he is, because the self-revelation there made is what God waits for, and from it springs an ever new relationship of vision and love. God shows God what he does, and, in manifesting his activity, manifests himself; he shows the activity of his divine nature in what he does, awaiting acknowledgement and agreement, for that mutual revelation and communication is the perpetual source of further manifestation. God is no static Being, but Life continuing eternally.

For God it is beatitude to manifest himself to God. The God who sees would, of course, humanly speaking, have the power to see, even without being shown; as, for example, God sees the sins of men who hide from him, like Adam. But in God there is the blessedness of showing himself and the blessedness of beholding what is shown, the joy of the mutual communication which comprises both the showing and the acceptance of the shown.

God, then, stands over against himself in the attitude of

God, an attitude that always reflects and springs from the essential Now of eternity, an attitude of trust, gratitude, surrender and acceptance. When the Son at Easter instituted confession, he wanted to bring this attitude of God within the reach of men, impart to them something of the life of the Trinity. And, to make this attitude a true one, he chose sin as the thing to be manifested. For sin is, ultimately, what man deceives himself about least. It is, at the same time, what has estranged him from God, and what must be recalled to mind if a man wants to see where he stands, how far off in relation to God. God uses the very cause of Adam's downfall, the very thing that alienated him from God, to draw him back again.

If we understand the Father as the Begetter, the Son as the Begotten, and the Spirit as proceeding from both, then we also understand that each Person has to be, wholly and exclusively, what he is, if the exchange within the one divine nature is to be possible. Each Person is wholly himself for the sake of the others, and for their sakes manifests himself to them completely. Out of gratitude to the Father the Son shows himself to him as his Begotten, in an attitude that is the archetype of confession; and he awaits the return-manifestation of the Father, in order to direct himself ever anew according to him. So, in confession as ordained by the Son, we aim at opening ourselves fully, acknowledging ourselves as what we are, so as to experience God equally fully, and out of this experience to order our lives anew.

Confession, being the gift of the Son, the fruit of his Passion, bears his imprint upon it: it is a revelation of the Father, a part of the gift the Father makes us in the Son, and it enables us to share in the attitude of the Son to the Father. The Spirit that proceeds from Father and Son, will, by his action in the sacrament, reveal something of the properties of both, and so proclaim his own Person. And what he reveals he also effects, both in the attitude of the penitent and in that of the confessor, through whom he speaks and forms the penitent.

The Son's open attitude, his "confession", to the Father it is not difficult to see and follow, both because he lived as man before us, and because he was born of the Father alone, the expression of the Father and the response to him. The attitude of the Spirit is, perhaps, harder to grasp, because he proceeds from both and his personal being is not intelligible to us. It may, however, be seen in the conjunction of the official and the personal rôles in the confessor, as indeed in the whole process of confession. As to the Father, we can say of his attitude that it is the source of that of the Son and the Spirit: it is what is primordial in the Godhead, the will from the beginning to reveal himself in the generation of the Son and the breathing-forth of the Spirit, in order to make manifest what God really is.

The Son's Life is a Continual Confession

All the sacraments are mirrored in the life of Christ; there they find their truth and archetypal image. If, at the end of his mission on earth, he instituted the sacrament of confession, it was because he saw in it, in a special manner, the fruit of his whole earthly life. Through it, in fact, he continues to work redemption from sin in all times. His whole life, therefore, from the beginning, is illuminated by the light of this sacrament. Even his eternal pact with the Father, to become man and redeem the world, included confession in a special manner: confession of sin, contrition on the part of man, and absolution on the part of God.

We might say that he lived on earth before the Father in the state in which the perfect penitent should live before his confessor, before the Church, and before God himself: in absolute openness, hiding nothing, always ready to be moved by the Holy Spirit, drawing assurance not from himself, but from the Father and his Spirit. The Son lived in a continuous community of feeling with the Father, expressed in his words: Not my will, but thine be done.

From eternity he saw the world's guilt, its pride and revolt, saw all its abominations. He saw man's alienation from the Father, a state brought about by sin; and, becoming man, he lived as one of the alienated. The world on which he entered was unchanged, at first, by his coming. He was just one of the estranged. Had he intended merely to live as God, he would, from the outset, have made his own appearance and manner of life utterly disparate from the others, the cleavage would be marked and enduring, and so his absolute otherness would have been plain for all to see. But his will was to be man among men, his appearance was to be no different from ours, he lived under like conditions. And the more he, as man, grew in the knowledge of sin, seeing and sensing the sinfulness of his fellowmen, the greater the burden of sin he, knowing and suffering, took upon himself, so that the Father, looking on him, saw also the increasing load of the world's guilt. So it was that he who knew the truth of sin was the same person who confessed it in truth. In the Son there is no disjunction between knowing and confessing, because all that he has and knows belongs to the Father. But since in knowing sin he bears it himself – for his knowledge of evil is simply passive experience, there is no question of it being active – he suffers on its account, yet not in any estrangement from God, but in his openness to him, which is essentially the same as the open confession through the word.

When a sinner confesses his guilt in confession, there arises a twofold relation between him and his sin: he identifies himself with his sin in recognizing and confessing it, and he affirms himself to be a sinner. And while he acknowledges it as his own and his own exclusively, he sets himself apart from it by his contrition. It is precisely his act of fully accepting his sin in confession and of sorrow for it that leads to its complete removal. The sinner confesses in order that the sin may be taken away. He joins himself with it, in order that he may be freed from it.

The Son too, in acknowledging sin, takes it on himself, but as something alien; and, in taking it on himself, he does not set himself apart from it. In fact, his acceptance of it is his way of striving to go to the point of identification with it. In approaching ever more closely to the Father he approaches more and more closely to man as sinner; it is a single movement whose purpose is to show sin to the Father and hand it over to him. When the sinner confesses his sin and, by his aversion from it and contrition, dissociates himself from it, he is freed from it and clothed in divine grace, whereas at the moment of committing the sin, he was not in grace. But then the Son takes sin on himself, he sends on it, from the outset, the rays of his own grace, and the Father sees in this acceptance of sin the Son's love in all its splendour. The Father is no longer able to see sin, when borne by the Son, in isolation, but only in its conjunction with the grace of the Son.

When a person confesses, he is enabled thereafter to begin a new life. Set loose from sin, he will be freer for God and God's word that he hears in confession. The Son resembles the penitent who aspires to a new life, in that the Son has received from the Father the office of bringing to the new men the new life, the new covenant. To do this, he must in no way remove himself from this new life; not only in not sinning (which, as God, he cannot do), but rather in adhering so closely to the will of the Father that even his human experiences, his experiences of sin and the world, which he knows on earth differently from in heaven, come wholly within the sphere of this will. He can and may gather to himself no human experiences that do not fit in with the way the Father in heaven experiences sin. He neither can nor will stand before the Father as knowing sin better than he, through being incarnate. Just as the penitent, who knows how and why he sinned, may not claim to know more about sin than the confessor, but has to subject himself in loyalty to the truth of the Spirit that the confessor points out to him. The Son cannot say to the Father: Now that I have become flesh, I am better able to judge how little blame attaches to much that men do, for thy creature is indeed weak. Or: I could perhaps have given back thy truth broken and darkened, because men, in their sin, are more capable of receiving thy truth broken than in its entirety. Or, perhaps in matters that concern the cross: It would be better, for the time being, to take on myself only a part of the suffering of the cross, and to go only to a certain point of endurance, so as to make such an impression on my followers and the rest of the world as is sufficient to keep them from sin; I could then go on living with them, and perhaps, if necessary, repeat the same later in a more intense degree. Or else: It would be better to have one crucified in every place where faith penetrates, so as to arouse attention everywhere. . . . And much else that might occur to the human mind and is equally inadmissible.

There can be no retreat from complete sacrifice, from death without restrictions. This means for the Son unreserved submission in hearing the Father. It means, equally, confession without adventitious colouring, unaffected by any human considerations, any proneness to certain sins that seem to the one concerned personal or excusable, as is often the case with penitents. The Son wills perfect truthfulness before the Father; he will not permit himself to be affected by any manoevre on the part of the sinner. Judgment, assessment, degree of gravity he leaves entirely to the Father to the point that, at the darkest moment, the Son understands him not at all. But it is precisely in renouncing all power to understand that he shows how pure and perfect and unceasing is his confession on the cross. It is not one in which both sides share the direction; that he leaves to the Father alone.

On the cross he receives absolution for his whole life, for all the sins he has borne, but this happens only at the moment of death, that is at the time when what he has done as man is no longer present to his spirit. He has borne our guilt so fully that he has included in it the possibility of being made excommunicate; even those reserved sins which cannot be absolved here and now he has taken on himself. He does not confess mankind's guilt with the feeling that it will be at once removed, that all will be made good immediately. It is part of his terrible burden that, in spite of his utter openness to the Father, he may not know this relief. Nor does he presume on his right to receive absolution and to taste its sweetness. He confesses and leaves it at that. He does not confess on the sole condition of then receiving absolution. So it is that Easter does not follow immediately on Good Friday, but the mystery of Holy Saturday comes in between.

People often confess as if they looked on confession and absolution as standing in a relationship of *do ut des,* accepting the unpleasantness of the procedure in anticipation of a relief due to them as of right. The Church meets them in this, by demanding from them that indifference of the Lord in respect of certain clearly defined sins only. She spares sinners any uncertainty while their sins are weighed and considered in the confessional. The confessor has, in fact, the right, the duty even, to examine and judge, and, accordingly, to delay or not, to bind or to loose. The sinner, however, ignores this right and demands absolution. But the heavenly Father has himself, in a way, delayed, in interposing the mystery of Holy Saturday. The Son hanging on the cross, did not throw aside his mortal vesture at once in order to put on the Father's glory to which he had a right. On the contrary, he went from the confession of the cross to the darkness of hell.

Incarnation

In the Incarnation, the Son, as the seed of God, commits himself to the operation of the Holy Spirit. It is as if he assumed one of the characteristics of the Spirit to breathe where he wills. The Son, indeed, plays the part of the Saviour of Israel, as was announced by the angel, but he does so by placing himself at another's disposition. The account of the Annunciation makes it appear as though everything transpired between Mary and the Holy Spirit, carried through by the intermediary of the angel, who speaks of the child to be conceived as if the latter had absolutely nothing to say in the matter. Mary's assent to the angel, too, is an assent to God, and there is no mention of her personal suitability or of the Son's choice of her. She surrenders herself in the fulness of her being, in a way corresponding to the Son's self-giving in the fulness of his sonship to the will of the Father and the impulse of the Spirit. Even though the Son knows all from the very beginning, this knowing does not concern him. He allows the Spirit to arrange everything.

There we see the basic disposition that later emerges in the mystery of confession. The Incarnation is itself a pre-confession in that the child, who will later make the more complete and comprehensive confession, makes himself, by becoming man, an instrument for redemption. He becomes one who is predestined to confessing; in that, too, he is made like to us, who are all conceived and born in order, one day, to confess our sins, both original and actual. We, however, are left free to choose whether to do this or not; but the Son confesses, because he has become man. For he became man, because he was to be the redeemer, to make confession. Yet in that he is like a human child in allowing others a right over himself, as a child is conceived at the will of others without knowledge of his fate. The initial attitude of the Son is to be his enduring and final attitude; just as there is nothing in the life of the Lord or any saint or any believer that was no part of the whole structure, foreshadowing the rest, and of a piece with it. The Son, in submitting to the law of human existence, sets his stamp on the lives of all who belong to him. He submits himself to this law like the fragment of earth that in the hands of the Father became Adam, as does every man who originates from the conjunction of two cells; but man's act of submission gains eternal significance only through being fused in that of the eternal Son.

Conception and Birth of Christ

The Son comes into the world, but not as a grown man straightaway to embark on a brief course of action and take away the world's guilt. Nor does he come merely for the hours or days of his Passion, to take on himself the sins of the world as a burden to which, as man, he could have had no relationship, not having gone the course of men. Then sin would have been like an insurmountable obstacle, which he would have taken on himself, a superhuman burden under which to die.

On the contrary, he wills to be completely man, and so chooses the complete human course, to be conceived, carried and born of a woman, and to pursue, as a child, an ordinary human life, until his hour strikes. For the mother who conceived him he is both the world's redeemer and a growing child, a child like all other children and yet the eternal Son who in eternity has decided to take on himself the burden of the world. This double character has its counterpart in the mother, for in bearing him, she bears, in her ordained and predestined fashion, the burden one day to be laid on her son. She bears her son as any mother bears her first child, and yet she must, in spirit, be prepared through her Son to bear the sin of the world. She knows in faith what is at issue. She knows sin from her surroundings; she has an exact understanding of the outrage to God. When she begins to bear the Son within her, sin is no longer merely external to her, since he who will bear the whole of sin dwells within her. It is as if she bore in herself the total confession of sin. With every sin she encounters, she knows that too is what he comes for, that he will take it on himself, that he will die for it. And when she gives birth to him at Christmas, she gives birth to the plenitude of absolution; indeed, the act of giving birth itself means an outpouring of absolution, for she is suddenly brought, as never before, into the presence of an exuberance of God's grace. Till then, she carried grace hidden within her; it had surrounded her in the breathing of the Spirit, but was not known by her as she knows it now, seeing it with her eyes and feeling it with her hands. This new state is akin to what God wills for man as a result of confession, through his sudden and incomprehensible emergence from sin to the fulness of grace, and that by a way preordained, yet miraculous, as the Lord's birth is itself a human way, yet miraculous. And as, for the sinner, the way is opened up through confession and contrition, it is, likewise, opened up through the sinless mother by her assent and obedience in bearing the Son. In this assent of hers she confesses both her previous and subsequent life; in it she makes acquaintance with sin, as the sinner knows sin in repenting of it. From contrition the mother comes to know a certain kind of anguish, anguish on account of the Son whose life is menaced by sin.

All the same, in making her own life the fulfilment of her Son's, she experiences the same kind of joy as absolution brings. The presence of the child that she sees and hears, that she has waited for, is for her the whole content of the Christian life, is how the joy of a mother that she will afterwards, at Easter, know as the joy of a bride, and communicate, in the Church, to all restored to grace and absolved from sin. This joy is utterly her own, yet one she will experience anew in those who confess; a joy that is not apart from that merited by the cross, since it is available to all, and thereby possesses its own perfect unity. Her joy is not distributed piecemeal; it is the one joy of the whole Church, which gives absolution in the name of God present within it. And the mother's participation in the birth of her own child is like the Church's participation in granting absolution to the world, the participation of those who absolve and of those who are absolved.

It is not possible to demarcate precisely the part played by the mother from that of the Son, especially as the Father and the Holy Spirit have each their part. Just as the joy all share is not divisible among them, so the part of the Father, Son and Spirit and that of the mother sharing in the work of redemption are not separable. The boundaries merge, and what stands out is always the unity of grace.

The Son, of course, is singled out to be conceived by an immaculate mother through the overshadowing of the Holy Spirit. This privilege is the sign, formerly only visible to the Father, that he is the eternal Son. It is, besides, what the Father gives Mary as a free gift in view of her future assent, and in her given to all men as a mysterious zone where God encounters them, as the place where the Incarnation can be accomplished. It is the irrational element accompanying the rational in his birth, the divine element present and active in the human. It is, too, a kind of alleviation of the work of the Son, who is to save the whole world, and who, in the mystery of his Incarnation, acquires various means to make the mysteries of the Father more accessible to men. At the same time, it is a certain aggravation of his burden, because he immediately brings those closest to him, Mary and Joseph, into a difficult situation, forces them into a greater concern with the supernatural aspect of the mysteries, and because the manner of his Incarnation makes clear that his divinity remains unimpaired. It is just as impossible to pass over the mystery of his conception through the Spirit and that of the virgin-birth as to pass over the mystery of his resurrection and ascension. In his conception he shows that anyone who concerns himself with the man Jesus is bound at once to come up against his divinity, and that what we can understand of the Son lies embedded in what is incomprehensible.

When a sinner is born, no one, of course, thinks of confession; but, in the course of his life, he will have to make a decision about it. The Son's conception and birth are related to his institution of the sacraments, which will follow infallibly. In the course of his life ending with the cross, the Son gathers to himself an increasing burden of sin; but the Father prepared his birth so that he should be untainted by sin, and thereby predestined him as the man able to know, bear and confess all men's sins. Were he born in a different manner, subject to original sin, his subsequent work of assuming man's sins would be lightened by reason of his own sinfulness. The period of our own conception, of our dwelling in the womb, of infancy without knowledge of good and evil, are conditioned by original sin. The Son, however, is wholly free; and this freedom of his is not simply due to his divinity, it is made visible in the way of his coming as man, so that the redeemed, who will be concerned in his confession on the cross through giving him their sins to bear and acknowledging him as redeemer and founder of the New Covenant, will be able to know him at his coming, and make the requisite confession of his being both divine and human.

Childhood

The Son's childhood, though sheltered by the purity of his mother and the holiness of his foster-father, is, in other respects, like that of any other child. His mother surveys all he does and his development, like any other mother. It is only when she sees him concerned about evil and its reality that she cannot provide an explanation by pointing out his own faults, but only by indicating the universal fact that man is inescapably prone to evil, both inflicting and suffering it. Yet it becomes clear to her that, as Messias, he needs a knowledge of evil, and that she must not conceal anything from him. And through the mother's gaze God the Father sees how the Son looks on sin and suffers in anticipation, how, with each new experience of human sin, he makes his earthly experience tally with the experience of God in heaven.

A Christian mother teaching her child what evil is and the gravity of sin has confession in mind. When Mary claims from her Son complete openness, she understands it to be the openness of the Son to God. Yet she is careful about his openness to her, for this care is a part of her duty as mother, like teaching him how to fasten his shoes.

Openness of the Son means showing what gives him pleasure and what pain, his knowledge of good and evil. He knows what belongs to Mary's function as mother, makes his state known to her, and shows her, likewise as her child, where the sphere begins of being alone with the Father. With his mother he will see that she desires what is good, but, when her human limitations show themselves, he points to what lies beyond her view perhaps vaguely and in the simple words of a child.

The clearest case of this is when, at twelve years of age, he draws very clearly the line between God's claims and those of his parents; and, in his instruction of the doctors, he makes known to them things beyond the reach of his parents. It is like an ordinary child who goes of his own accord to confession; he cannot very well tell his parents, when he gets home, all that was said in the confessional. He has learnt to take the place assigned to him in the sphere which is essentially that of God and so introduces into his life a new tension; this, however, is a blessing for the parents too, even when there are things they cannot grasp. Here the personal character of confession stands out most clearly, safeguarded by the authority of the Church. The parents of Jesus know that he belongs to God. They cannot expect to find him elsewhere than where God is. Even in the midst of their natural uneasiness, due to their human limitations, they cannot think that any harm has happened to him (for he is only at the beginning of his mission), or that he has been led astray to evil (for he is God's Son).

He is so submissive to God's guidance that he must always do what God wills. To God belongs absolute priority. In that he has no need of the advice of his parents, for his sinlessness is assured. On occasion, then, there will be a violent collision between the two authorities, not unlike that which Christian parents may experience in the spiritual guidance given by a priest to their child even more so than through his influence in confession. The life of Mary and Joseph was so deeply rooted in custom that Christ would undoubtedly, have had to count on their opposition, had he told them beforehand that he would stay in the temple to teach the scribes. It would have been humanly incomprehensible to them, and, in spite of their holiness, they would have wanted to prevent him, just because they were grown-up persons. Two results might have followed: that they would have combated the Son's mission and have impeded it perhaps in a decisive matter. So the Son had no choice. The shock he gave his parents arose through his abrupt revelation to them of the full extent of his relation to the Father, which bound him far more stringently than that to his parents. Take the case of a highly conscientious child whose parents are not particularly zealous in matters of religion. He may well have to confess things in which they are concerned, and they may try to deter him. The comparison is not exact, but it does apply to some extent. The unbelieving parents, then, would have to reconcile themselves to this, without understanding it. So it is with the Lord's parents, believers though they were. He had merely done his primary duty.

What he knows as man comes, more or less, within the scope of his parents' understanding, just as a child's sins and shortcomings are clear to his parents. But once the child begins going to confession, although they may have some idea of the kind of things he speaks about, they have no knowledge of the inner aspect of confession, which derives from the soul baring itself utterly before God. The confessor, in his official capacity, will perhaps read into the child's confession much more than the parents could, because of his experience; just as the scribes, listening to what Jesus said, had a much better idea of his actual knowledge than his parents, whose understanding was limited by their lack of learning.

The words used by the Son to justify himself – "Did you not know that I must be about my Father's business?" – are both a defence and a demarcation. They are a defence of his mission. A child's mother might consider it useful for his education for her to know exactly what takes place in his confession; but the child himself must maintain secrecy. The Lord, in fact, by his conduct creates a precedent for others to follow. But for children the right of confession means a sudden plunge into a new world; and henceforth it is right that they should no longer have to tell their parents everything. The Church's exclusive authority in confession is justified in that man there learns to stand before God as a more independent and responsible being. For that reason, attempts (as in the Moral Rearmament movement) to exact confession of sins outside the sphere of authority are bound to fail. Confession is not, primarily, an affair between men, but between men and God, and the Church, which watches over the rights of God, may not keep a child from confession just because he gets on perfectly with his parents. Some things there are, and bound to be, which transcend the sphere of human social relations, and the time comes when the child understands this as a matter of course.

So it is that the conduct of the twelve-year-old Christ brings out in clear relief the sphere of the Father. Previously, this was, in a way, hidden in the foreknowledge of his mother and foster-father. These two, in spite of their uneasiness, must find peace in a deeper understanding, when they see that what happened was in the line of his mission.

Baptism in the Jordan

What is established here is the determination of the time for confession, something very difficult to grasp. When is the time for confession? The time, say, for a General Confession? When to make one's confession in such a way that the confessor may decide the course to be followed in the future? There is, in fact, a time when, as a result of a new insight into confession, one makes a completely fresh start, sees everything in its origin, understands everything as a new and special indication of God's will, even though, as with the Son, one had never become alienated from God. There is even a time to give special importance to the confession of another – in this case, John's – and to make it a decisive factor in one's own life.

The time was made known through John the Baptist, and therein a new element entered the Son's attitude of confession as regards the Father. It was the event the Son was waiting for, and one that had to be initiated, not by him, but by the Baptist. He, the Son, had only to respond. It was as if two persons were charged with founding an Order, and, all at once, one says to the other: "I will come out into the open now, and see if I find any followers", and so acts in obedience to his charge; then the hour has struck for the other also. The Son knew at that moment that John had confessed, for his part; he had decided to terminate his mode of living hitherto, and had begun to make straight the way of the Lord in obedience to the Father, his own Father-confessor as it were. This obedience could not be other than right, and so the Son accepted all that it involved. He himself entered into the Baptist's situation in his confession, so as to draw the same conclusion as John. John had not undertaken a work of which the Son could say: I certainly did not charge him to do it, but let us see how it turns out, and then it will appear if it is right ....

Instead, the Son was placed under an absolute obligation through the work initiated by John, because it was a work of confession, and the Son came to institute confession; because it was a work of obedience, and confession and obedience are bound up with one another, and the Son came to be obedient unto death. He had therefore, to join himself to John's obedience, in order to accomplish his own obedience to death.

The Son, indeed, was to die on the cross to atone for all men's sins, and yet he initiated, on the cross, a way of following the cross-bearer. So did the Father, in spite of the Son's unique, complete and perfect mission, initiate for him something like a following of the Baptist's mission, which preceded him.

Those who live in a contemplative Order are protected in various ways. The regular routine of choir, silence, contemplative prayer is always recalling God's greatness and presence, and facilitates conformity to his will. The "active" life demands more rapid, certain and frequent contact with God, so as to remain within the sphere of his will; and here even slight infidelities may have disastrous effects on one's special task as a Christian. There is a corresponding difference as regards confession in the two kinds of life. The baptism in the Jordan was an intervention of the Baptist's active life in the Lord's contemplative life now ending. The child of twelve had gone of his own accord, of course, in unison with the Father's will. The man of thirty, on the contrary, went on the initiative of John (equally in accord with the Father). The Son was wholly amenable to the sign conveyed by John's action, though, in his human capacity, perhaps he had no knowledge that John had to give it him. That kind of sign is what we expect saints in the Church to give, but it should also be looked for in every confession. It may come from both together, as when, for instance, the confessor accompanies his injunction, adequate in itself, with a reference to the example of some saint. John, when he began baptizing, acted under the impulse of the Holy Spirit. He heard and accepted God's word, which lived in him as it does in the saints; and that word made of him a sign for the Lord. John had already taken on the Lord's life of action according to the Father's will, and, in that way, interrupted the Lord's contemplation; yet it can be said that the Lord's contemplative period reached its culmination in the start of John's action, so that there is one prayer common to both, contemplative in the case of the Lord, active in that of John.

Confession as an act does not stand in isolation, but sums up and gives visible expression to an attitude that should never be discarded; just as every action should flow from contemplation, and contemplation should always comprise readiness at any time to be sent out on some action. That is what we mean by "indifference"; it is a disposition at all times to receive from God a sign, either to continue in prayer or to break it off for some activity. The actual waiting before the confessional for the Church's intimation and order is itself simply the visible expression of a continuous waiting in readiness for confession for the moment when the act of confession will be posited, the moment appointed by the Spirit.

In this moment when disposition and act overlap there must be the greatest possible readiness for the intimation given by the Spirit, because it also involves another's function. Before John began to baptize, the Son stood before the Father in a sublime solitude, which had its own special quality of permanence. The Son held himself ready and submissive each day as on the day before, and as he would the next. But once the active mission of the Baptist began, it entered into the Son's prayer to the Father, for John baptized in view of the Son's coming. This presence of it in the Son's prayer demanded of him a different kind of attentiveness, which extended to John's mission and office. The

Son's openness to the Father may be considered his continuous attitude of confession. John's office was one of complete authority over the Son, and its intervention means that the Son's state of expectancy was translated into an act, a decision.

Baptism is purification. John's baptism presupposed confession of sinfulness, and, in the baptism of Christ's institution, purification was to mean complete absolution from sin. But when a man comes with authority to cleanse from sin and exercises this authority over the Son, then the Son is to him as one obliged to confess. When, then, Jesus had himself baptized, he put himself among sinners in need of absolution, and, therefore, on the way of the cross, where he would bear the sins of all and confess them to the Father. John in the discharge of his function initiated this active progress to the cross, seeing the Lord as the Lamb without sin who takes away the guilt of the world.

Temptation

The Lord tempted in the desert knew perfectly that he *could* overcome the devil simply by showing him how much more powerful was God than he. At a deeper level, however, he knew that he could only conquer by letting himself be tempted without yielding in the least, and instead making clear to the tempter his abiding with the Father, his obedience to his mission. To live a life of untarnished obedience, even in the certainty that both temptation and tempter persist, means to live in the Father's presence. That is loyalty to the Father's mission, a loyalty which, it would seem, only has meaning to the Father. From an earthly standpoint, such obedience seems a waste of strength; for, had the Son yielded in some way to temptation, he could have taught the devil something — but this too would have been meaningless, and doubly so in that one cannot teach the devil anything. Therefore, the Son chose weakness, which is strength in the Father. But the Father himself had no need of this manifestation of weakness on the part of the Son, since he knew that the Son would be obedient always and up to death. None the less, he willed to accept this declaration of obedience, not indeed to strengthen the Son's obedience, but to bring out a certain pointlessness in that obedience, so that the Son would feel it, as it were to be his proper element, and see how it led directly to the cross, submitting to it in that light. His object was that we, who came after, should not, in our slight, insignificant temptations, look for strength in ourselves, but in the Son, and not him alone but in the Father too, through the Holy Spirit of divine obedience.

The hidden foundation of this obedience lies in God; at the most, we can only have some inkling of it. But when we find this divine obedience as practised in the gospel, we know that the Son did not keep it simply for himself, but put something of it into his confession. We see him standing fast against sin in God's presence, contemplating the way that lies ahead, and this attitude of his, calm and undisturbed, is the outcome of his victory over the devil. And this victory is not achieved by overwhelming force, but by a calm refusal of the temptation, spoken to the Father as well as to the tempter himself. In so far as it is addressed to the Father, it becomes an element in the grace intended by the Father for men as an effect of the cross, a grace hardly at all perceptible, but whose effect is to make of life a unified whole. The Father sends the Son his Spirit, so as to be always with him in the Spirit. The Son on the cross breathes forth his Spirit back to the Father, but the Spirit still remains as it were in the background, always present to create unity in each man's life.

Before the Lord handed over the power to bind and loose to his apostles, he had experienced the depth and range of temptation. In so doing, he laid up for man a capital resource for anyone to draw on in moments of weakness. What he was specially aware of was that whoever would walk the way of confession, which is pre-eminently a way of the cross, would be called to pause and reflect before God; and for this he would draw on the same capital of the Lord's temptation. For the sinner must withstand the temptation to continue sinning, and this pause and break in sinning is the first stage of the reflection and conversion that leads to confession. Only if he starts from this point can he be taken back again into grace; and the way from this point to the grace of absolution leads through the experience, inexpressible in words, undergone by the Son before the Father in the Holy Spirit between the desert and the cross. It is inexpressible, because the accompanying action of the Father is so discreet yet efficacious, and because the Son's obedience comprises each particular laid down in the Old Testament, fulfilling all, point by point, in the unwavering constancy that is the special quality of his obedience, up to his death on the cross, and the Father fulfils the promise by raising him to life. This constancy in obedience that omits nothing, that wills to experience everything up to death on the cross, is the chalice he drinks to the dregs, at the very time too when he prays it might pass from him. It is the chalice that contains the fulness of bitter experience, its rounded shape, representing obedience, encompassing all the sins of the world. There they are in the place where God willed to bring them, in the state of being drunk by the Son. His own state is an image of communion; for he lets his body die through men's sins, so that all who were sinners may receive a share in him and his new life. But, for sinners to be able to follow his way, he has to know the place of temptation, in order to find again, in the weakness of one tempted, strength for his own life, the strength to recover the way which leads to confession.

Public Life

The Son's entrance on his public life contains an element of the examination of conscience. He had always kept heaven and the Father before his eyes, the purity of eternal life, and in this life he saw whatever on earth departed from it, all misconceptions of the Father's nature and purposes, every deliberate breach with him, all that obscured or destroyed faith, hope and charity. All this he saw in his love for men, but this love did not impair the clearness of his vision. The discrepancies he saw were always present to his consciousness. In knowing sin, its motives and effects, he was like other men, who, through being bound to the body, have an intimate knowledge of temptation and its various forms. Yet, at the same time, being purity and charity itself, he knows separation from God primarily through his own closeness to God. In this way of knowing sin, the Son resembles someone who understands his sins in the light of the Holy Spirit, and sees where he has to begin his admission of them; someone who never wearies of looking everywhere to see how he has failed, so as to avow it correctly. The Son, then, went into the world and passed through it as one gathering up sin in view of confessing it. He gathered it, inasmuch as he was constantly taking it on himself, and, at the same time, continuously effacing it; his action here being parallel with that of the penitent with his resolutions. When someone has committed some definite sin, he sees exactly the departure from the norm, is sorry for it, is ready to confess it and to accept penance. All this he can do in close dependence on the Lord, who knows the sin more exactly than anyone else, who draws the sinner's attention to it, who perhaps reproaches him for his own good, warns him so as to prevent relapse into the sin, baptizes or absolves and thereby wholly effaces it, who yet, in each case, whether he absolves or not, takes the sin on himself, and, in bearing it, confesses it to the Father and takes on the penance for it.

The Son, then, lived patiently with the cross in view, and his patience grew as the burden of sin weighed more heavily on him. His will and charge was to bear all our sins, and these he showed the Father, who was always present with him, though he could not die on the cross then and there. And just as the consciousness of sin should not be blunted by the postponement of confession, but made more acute, and as such postponement ought to be a sign of fervour and not of indifference, so the Son felt the burden he carried more and more acutely, was more and more conscious of its varied nature. He felt each kind of sin in its own special way; each caused its own pain. He was man, and man is vulnerable to suffering on many levels, for he can suffer from himself or his surroundings, in body or in soul, from heat or cold, from fatigue or tension, in all his organs, whether he is conscious of them or not, and in regions of the soul he had never suspected. The range of the Son's suffering corresponded to the whole compass of his human nature.

Desert and Mount of Olives

The two great sections of our Lord's life are generally looked upon as two distinct stages, in the first of which he grew and developed in body and mind, and learnt as man to know the Father and to grow into his mission. In prayer and contemplation he learnt to know the heavenly Father and his own divine nature, in order to enter on his life of action from a fully-developed awareness. The sharp separation of the two parts is, however, belied by the forty days in the desert; for, when the decision to begin his active life had already been taken and put into effect, the Son put himself once again into the Father's hands to be moulded and shaped like clay, underwent the short active experience of a renewed testing in prayer, and delivered himself over to be tempted by Satan. All this happened while he was weakened by his forty-days' fast, in order that, in his weakness, he might come forth victorious from his conflict with the devil, and, as a conqueror, and at the same time a weak man, tread the path of action. He had behind him the experience of all that can keep man back from working for God and God alone, summed up as it is in the three temptations. He proceeded along his way, inwardly changed by this experience, which he kept ever with him, so as to renew it at the hour of his Passion. The Mount of Olives was also contemplation, but no longer in order to lead to action, nor to obtain strength to act rightly; it was contemplation unto death, restoration to the Father of all his active powers, so as to be able to suffer in the way the Father wished; so as to suffer unhindered by any thought of action.

If we look on the Son's whole attitude on earth as one of perfect love for the Father in complete openness before him, as an attitude of confession, we can see how, within it, the events in the desert and on Olivet mark an important cleavage. On those two occasions, the will of the Father was accepted anew and explicitly. All the rest of the time that Christ lived among men, whether in the quiet of the family or the activity of the apostolate, he took on himself the sins he encountered, sins of all kinds, in the setting of his human experiences. He was the Son of God, bearing them in his human form. But at these two junctures he put himself in the hands of the Father, so that the Father could act on him directly and give him the burden to bear that he wished.

When a man's strength is exhausted and his fatigue extreme, ordinary human experience is sufficient for him to judge easily and almost unconsciously what is still "humanly possible", and what is too much. And it was because the Son, in bearing man's sins, knew and experienced this fatigue, as he knew all other human states that he went into the desert and on to the Mount of Olives. The time up to those events represents the time of "virtue", when one is resolved to endure, the will is set in readiness for what is to come. Subsequently, it is the time of fatigue and exhaustion, when the human powers fail, and one has to seek afresh a relationship to God. It is a wonderful thing to be resolved in advance and to pray for courage, say before martyrdom or torture; afterwards, in the midst of the flames or torments, one should not merely have no desire of escape, but should stay in God's presence, find him anew in suffering. The Son willed to show the Father that, in his life of action, the Father's will was his direct concern as much as in his suffering. His active life might appear to us the expression of his intense desire to take on the burden of men's sins, a life so conducted that there was no call for the Father to intervene by any reproach or directive. But that was not how the Son acted; every step he took was indicated beforehand by the Father, and taken in his presence. Besides this, there were particular occasions when he awaited his Father's intervention, rather as a confessor should always be given the right and the possibility of interrupting the penitent's confession with a question or directive.

The changes, then, in the Son's attitude of confession were not due to any vacillation, but to a new encounter with the Father. These contemplative periods within the active life are like a general confession, in which the whole of one's past life is exposed to view for God to dispose it anew. "Is it, Father, as you intended? Am I carrying on in the way you want? Can I continue like this?" The constant state of confession of sins and acceptance of their burden is interrupted in order to be reassumed more perfectly. Yet, for the time being, there is no absolution given, for one must wait for the hour of the cross.

The temptation in the desert (and again that on the Mount of Olives, to let the chalice pass away) was, in part, caused by the Son's long fast and consequent weakness. He himself willed to show the Father, in his own person, how temptation from human sources comes about. But, at a deeper level, the temptation by the devil was a kind of answer by the Father to the Son's renewed gift of himself. It was the Father who plunged him down into the abyss of life as conditioned and formed by sin, a kind of life seat and occasion of which is the body and all that pertains to it.

3. THE CONFESSION ON THE CROSS

The Passion

THE MOMENT of the great purification has come. All his life, the Son, has, indeed, taken sin on himself; he has also forgiven sins when that was needed. But what was then effaced could only disappear through the grace of the cross to come. For the sinner in question his sins had been cancelled, but the Son had to bear them till the time of the cross. In addition, there were all the sins that were not to be effaced at the time; these he bore while they remained yet unchanged, their action unimpaired, even working their effect in him, rather as sin is active in the sinner. He too, in a certain way, was alienated from God by sin, not like the sinner whose sense for God is blunted, but in the form of heightened suffering. The suffering of feeling abandoned by the Father is the price he pays for sin.

It is as though, on his way to the cross and on the cross, he had to learn all about sin in its most subtle forms, and this through his body, in the first instance, through all the particular forms of pain it was given him to feel. The body, however, is the image of the soul and the way of access to it, in fact, to his very person, which he knew and felt was what all his sufferings aimed at: he, and he alone, as the appointed representative of the Father, was the target of each sin. Thus every element in the Passion heightened for him the necessity for the confession of the cross. If his alienation from God through sin had been like ours, inuring him to sin, then the cross would have had to teach him a different course. For there he encountered, not the individual, but the whole complex of sin, and this encounter, in the scenes of the Passion, deepened his idea of his destiny as Redeemer. Certainly, he was never tempted to understand his mission as a successive process that could be prolonged as he wished. Yet since the Father had so appointed, he needed suffering as a kind of final confirmation, in which all his individual actions were brought into a single whole, corresponding to the single unexpiated man of sin.

The penitent never, in fact, sees his sins in their entirety. He has thought out what to say, but, as he waits, while the woman, it may be, before him has still not finished, and the child behind him talks all the time, it occurs to him that he has forgotten his want of patience and charity that he ought to confess, and so has to renew his contrition so as to include these. In the same way, it is possible always to discover new, aggravating, circumstances of one's sins, and, with them, new sins may also come to light. One never quite strips oneself bare, there is always another layer to discard.

When the Son was scourged naked, and naked nailed to the cross, with the thorns and nails penetrating his flesh, it was then that he recovered the nakedness of the first man. In this, he had in view, not the state of sinlessness, but that of sin; for his arms embraced all that was, is and will be. It was all, in its utter reality, loaded on to him in his nakedness. And for him, denuded of all power, it was no longer possible to survey the entirety of his burden. For it was not something gradually accumulated in the course of his life; and so, on the cross, he could not master the burden by dividing it up. What he had taken on himself in a certain order suddenly turned against him like some ferocious external force, and he felt as if he had nothing in common with the burden he had prepared. It was some independent, anonymous force that broke over him, one that belonged nowhere. Each sin, however, had its own special barb pointed at him and inflicting its wound. His confession, at that moment, was like the utterance of a single word: All; while, from time to time, a single element would emerge and take shape before him, and then his cry would be: That too!

When he cried out: Father, why hast thou abandoned me? and: I thirst! that, too, was an expression of his confession charged with its intolerable burden. It expressed and answered the overwhelming force of sin that itself was the resounding reply to his question "why"? The Father was concerned in all that the Son showed him; but on the cross the Son was no longer aware of this. Thus the pentitent himself may have the impression that the confessor does not understand him any more, or feel so submerged by his sins that his very confessing seems pointless. There is always more to say, but the purpose of confessing has been lost to view, and the weight of sins leaves the soul breathless. So it was that the Son diverted to himself the arrows of sin aimed at the Father; but under the intensity of the assault on him he lost sight of his real purpose. Perhaps it was this sense of futility that killed him; for recognition of the purpose would be for him salvation from death.

It is certain that, all through his life, in the course of assuming men's sins, he felt contrition for each one of them. It was a source of grief to him that they had been committed and the Father offended. He suffered from the estrangement between the Father and the sinner, and as the mediator between them. But on the cross there was no further question of "between"; he was himself the man concerned, and on him lay the burden of sin. Contrition, then, was as if merged in the one general pain, which sprung from the direct encounter between confession and penance. Suffering overwhelmed and engulfed everything, even the act and feeling of contrition. Contrition would have meant that there was a common measure between sin and penance, that the bearing of sin corresponded to its gravity. Contrition demands, if it is to be posited as an act, a definite object; but on the cross there was no definable object any longer, just as the power of sin and the pain expiating it had become indistinguishable.

When the Lord, in his life on earth, met a sinner, he knew at once how things stood with him. On the cross, however, he experienced each one's sins in a quite different way, for there he had to bear them himself and suffer from them. Previously, he saw sin, man was an open book to him, and he could instruct the sinner and put him on the right way; but his own hour had not yet come. On the cross he made the experience of suffering, and something of that experience he laid up in the sacrament of penance. The movement by which someone carries his sins to the sacramental tribunal is, in a sense, comparable with that by which the Son carried all men's sins to the cross. There sin was something crude, unshaped, a kind of raw material, like the beams of the cross. No one can make his confession a sublime and lofty experience, any more than the sins borne on the cross had anything sublime about them. The priest hears sins and receives them, as commissioned by the Holy Spirit, somewhat as the Father accepted them on the order of the Son hanging on the cross.

The sacrament of penance has its completely objective side, in virtue of its relation to the Trinity. The act of confessing is, indeed, personal, but judgment and absolution are objective. In that way it is the reverse of the Eucharist, where, despite the sacramental character independent of man, and so objective, the Lord holds himself in a subjective condition; for here it is he who gives himself without reserve, while the person receiving is objective. In this twofold movement, with the sign reversed, a sacramental circle is completed, and we see how confession and communion belong together and mutually correspond.

The Church itself sees the two sacraments as connected in this way; and even those who occasionally find they have nothing to confess must still submit to confession of sin, since they belong to the community of sinners. They have, at least, to take part in bringing forward on their own account some of the burden of sin into the objective presence of God, and to receive from God the purification ordained in view of the Eucharist. The reception of communion, where man's part is objective, is infinitely less costly to him than confession; for he is, in truth the receiver, not the giver who gives himself utterly. It is the Lord, who makes the gift of himself, to whom this giving is costly. In this way, our slight effort in confession corresponds, though diminutive by comparison, with the infinite striving of the Lord, to the point of death, to give us his flesh and blood. It follows that, ultimately, it is not sin that chiefly prompts our human effort here; for in confession we acknowledge that we have understood something of what the Lord did for us on the cross, and continues to do at each communion.

The distinction between the subjective and objective factors is based on the Lord's twofold knowledge of sin. His knowledge of it before the cross is parallel with man's commission of sin. His knowledge on the cross, where he was overwhelmed by the weight of sin, is parallel with the sinner's confession, in which he is crushed by sorrow. For the Lord, his knowledge of sin in his lifetime was subjective (he saw it as man sees it), but on the cross it was objective (he saw it as it is in itself, before God).

Holy Saturday

From the standpoint of confession, we may look on the mystery of the descent from the cross as a summing-up by the confessor of all that had been said and enacted. It was as if the Father was setting before the Son's gaze all that he bore, but in a different form, linking his acceptance and acknowledgement of sin with its removal by absolution. The passion was over; all feeling had been taken away, but the joy of the accomplished task was not yet granted. Sin had become purely objective, independent of human estimation and feeling, divorced from any consideration of who had committed it. It was, purely and simply, sin heaped up and gathered into a whole, which must of necessity have unleashed the most frightful suffering, had not the Son's past suffering effected the separation of sin from sinner. But the sight of sin as it is in itself is no reason for rejoicing. It is simply the recognition of what in fact is, that the mass of sin is so deeply rooted and widespread; that is how it looks when seen apart from men, that is from both the sinner and the Lord. In this objective view is also to be seen the relation between man, temptation, sin, its gravity, a relation apparently clear and definite, but, in fact, not calculable.

In the sacrament of penance, after the confession and before the absolution, sin is there in an objective fashion, whether the confessor expressly sums it up in words, or, as judge and dispenser of grace, forms an interior image of what was confessed. He owes it to his office and to the penitent to present the sins objectively in this way. For the penitent also the content of his confession must be freed of all subjective aspects and appear in its intrinsic gravity. It is no longer a matter of how my sins seemed to me at the time, what the personal circumstances were, that I thought it was a grave matter, considered it sinful, that other matters were also involved but I am not sure if I was guilty, I wanted to mention it to make certain, and so on. Now, at any rate, all that is finished with; in a way it is like the transition from a patient's confused description of symptoms to the doctor's diagnosis. The penitent himself cannot fully grasp the diagnosis made, yet it brings him considerable relief. His groping, perhaps anguished, mind is given the answer it vainly sought, and God's representative takes the responsibility for it. The fibres binding the sin to the sinner, are no longer visible, although the absolution has not yet been given; even though the whole thing, from the standpoint of the confessor, may be graver than the sinner thought; though the penitent cannot rid himself of his involvement with the sin in its newly presented aspect.

For the Lord this encounter was particularly oppressive, for it was one between purity itself and sin itself. When, as man, he absolved someone from sin, for instance Mary Magdalen, he saw in the person absolved the effect of the absolution he gave. He suffered from the sin, but rejoiced over the cleansing. Suffering and joy each produced the other in mutual interaction. Here, however, all feeling on his part had ceased, there remained only a kind of objective experience of something fearful, only the state of being stifled and buried under the deadly load of the world's guilt.

If, in the Old Testament, mutual confession of sins had been attempted, then, at times, men would have come up against certain limits. One man might have confessed his sins to another from a need to talk about this side of his life and relation to God, possibly to see himself clearly or else to obtain counsel and help, or even to make the other know him better. It might all have been conducted in some measure of humility and detachment.

When, however, the Lord, after his resurrection, instituted confession for the first time, it was in virtue of the reality of his risen body, which as the price for this institution had gone through Good Friday and Holy Saturday. Even before his Passion, when he converted men to the following of him, when he cleansed Mary Magdalen from her sins, he sometimes took on himself as man a whole section of their confession. He placed his divine knowledge and love at the service of his human knowledge and love, forgave sins as a man who was, at the same time, God, offering the effect wrought to the Father, who retained it as something provisional till the day of the cross.

It was from the cross that the risen Lord, as bridegroom, imparted to the Church the full power of absolution, the Christian sacrament; also that confession was entirely a mystery and possession of the Son, his gift to men and the Father's to him. Because the Son on the cross had "confessed" the sins of the world to the Father, he entered into a new mystery as regards the world, one that remained hidden between his death and resurrection, and was carried with him in his progress through hell as an effect wrought by his Passion. The Son, therefore, had borne sin in two different ways. On Good Friday, till his death, he had borne it as the personal guilt of each individual, borne it with his divine and human being to expiate it in the most personal act the Son could perform for sinners. At that time each sin was seen as bound up with the person committing it; it bore his own features. On Holy Saturday, however, in his vision of the world's sin from the standpoint of the world below, sin was disengaged from the subject, the sinner, and took on the aspect of that monstrous enormity which constitutes the horror of the world below and fills him who contemplates it with repulsion. It was sin as finally and eternally inescapable, but become anonymous, from whose reality and aspect it was no longer possible to deduce the individual sinners and their share in it. Thus, in this passage through the world below there was something in the nature of a personal bearing (or an oppressive vision) of impersonal sin.

The risen Lord, knowing this twofold mystery, knew how fully the mystery of confession from then on belonged to him; for it was given him by the Father on account of the suffering he had undergone. His abandonment on the cross by the Father, his total separation from the Father in the world below, both belong to the core of the mystery of the "confession" he took on himself of the world's sin. His risen body had come forth from his crucified and buried body, just as his earthly body had come forth from the decision taken in heaven to become man. The new body given by the Father was that in which he returned unsullied to the Father. As applied to confession we might say that his earthly body was the body of his confession which had to bear both the personal sins of each individual, and also original sin and sin in itself. The risen body, however, was the body of his absolution which no longer had to bear sin, since that had been borne and everything atoned for on the cross. The former body had gathered up on to itself the perfect confession, whereas the latter one was a gift made to signify absolute forgiveness. Sin was being confronted; it needed no longer to be borne as by the other body. The risen body continues always to impart absolution from out of itself, indeed it gives itself in absolution, as it gives itself also in the Eucharist, in order that absolution, through its intimate union with the body of the believer, may attain its utmost efficacy and permanence.

Easter

The Son had promised that he would rise on the third day, a promise no one believed now. Even he was deprived, during the Passion, of his vision of the risen life; the knowledge and hope of it was withdrawn from him more and more. When he died and went down to hell, this withdrawal was complete. He went obediently to death, without looking to right or left; death left him no possibility of estimating its duration and the brevity of the time till the resurrection. It came like lightning; it was an instant absolution.

As far as the disciples were concerned, their grasp of the resurrection was by stages. First, their uncertainty and fear; then, through the news brought by the women, an oscillation between doubt and hope, till there came the sudden conviction that it was really he who was there. In that they finally experienced something of the suddenness of the resurrection.

A confession in which the mind is occupied all the time with the coming absolution is no following of the Lord. In confession and contrition the essential is to concentrate upon one's sins; and when confession is finished and responsibility handed over to the confessor, there is an implied renunciation of all right of disposition over oneself in respect of one's sins, an indifference to what God's representative may decide about the penitent. Absolution is not anticipated. It ought to come to the penitent like a flash of lightning. And though psychologically he needs time to be fully cognizant of it, for the joy it causes to flow into him by degrees, the joy of renewed contact with the

Trinity, although he needs time to make room in himself for this joy, still the interval is unimportant beside the sudden inrush of grace.

The Person of the Son had delivered himself up to his Passion so completely that, for him too, the resurrection meant renewed contact with the Father. During his suffering he had laid aside his divinity, placing it with the Father, and so the resurrection meant its recovery. But since he had suffered as man, his reunion with the Father was accompanied by the utmost joy in his human nature. The joy which he gave as a gift to mankind redeemed was not one he had not experienced himself. They were to participate in his joy through absolution, in his joy which filled to overflowing the human capacity for joy created with Adam, for, in the Son, it partook of the divine joy itself. That was the will of the Father, accepting the fulfilment of the Son's mission to the very end. For just as the Son had to confess sin for all and receive absolution in the place of all, so he experienced his joy, not only as present to himself, but as the joy of the redeemed; and this infinitely enhanced its value.

Absolution means that sin is completely taken away. The Son has borne man's sins. Their removal, however, is not a sort of negation, leaving a gap, but a positive holiness that radiates purity in a purified creation. This creation is now wholly the possession of the Father, by whom the Son had thought to have been abandoned. Absolution does not imply turning away from sin so much as turning to God; and the Son now sees in each one he has redeemed a dwelling of joy in whom he may live in fulfilment of the Father's commission. When he reveals himself so present in a man — "I no longer live, but Christ lives in me" — that assures him that he belongs to the redeemed possessed by the Father. In his death on the cross, Christ saw man as the sin which he bore, for he had breathed forth back to the Father his Spirit, the Holy Spirit of love; but now, all men are once again present to him, and once again he can dispose of his love, and all men are once more new, mature and capable of bearing fruit, living in the love of the Trinity.

The disciples had taken part in the earthly life of the Lord; they had experienced the mystery of his being Son of God, and had seen a number of his acts and other events which had astounded them. They never really understood what he foretold, but seized upon isolated sentences and interpreted them in the measure of their understanding. To them the Lord's death seemed a catastrophe, and it left them wholly unprepared for the resurrection. The Lord, however, knew the state of each of them, and gave them the explanation they needed to understand the meaning of his whole life and of every detail. This gave their own life its meaning too; and it was then that they received their mission to go out and proclaim the gospel, to continue, in fact, his own work according to his directions.

On Easter evening he summed up the meaning of his life in the words, "whose sins you shall forgive, they are forgiven". That is the what his teaching amounted to, nothing theoretical, for he had himself lived by it and acted accordingly; and, in this form as lived, he communicated his own being to the Church. His Incarnation was an act of pure love; throughout his life, he never departed from this love; and when we contemplate his life in the light of confession, love and confession are seen to coincide in him. He loved the Father's creation to the point of giving up his life for it; but he did so by assuming its sins, confessing them, and gaining absolution from the Father for its sake and in its place. He assumed human life so as to be able to give it up. This mission of love gave the highest glory to the Father, and this culminated in the Son making the Father's creation glorious. He glorified the Father by glorifying men in the Father; he took on human form to show the Father the glory of what was made by him. Something of the Father's was glorified by the Son in his life, in such a way that the Father experienced the glory of this something that belonged to him, that was taken out of him. This glorification, however, can only be effected by man remaining in the Father's love; which means remaining open to the Father: the openness of a whole life shown us by the Son, who, though burdened with sin, dying in dereliction, never for a moment abandoned his state of openness. This openness is the perfect attitude of confession, the gift he left to the Church.

4. THE INSTITUTION OF CONFESSION

The Appointment of the Apostles

It is a striking fact that the Lord never asked the apostles whether they were willing. On the evening of Easter, when they were all together, he appeared to them, and, in the midst of their rejoicing, gave them two commands: to receive the Spirit, and to forgive sins. They had reached a point where there was no further choice. Till then there had been little said about the Lord bearing sin, and little too about how the disciples were to act in regard to sinners. What was seen was the good news that was to put an end to sin, and the good example that had to be given, but what the Lord had said about conduct as regards sin applied to all believers as much as to the apostles. The command, however, given that Easter Day all at once put them in a quite different position; they were no longer merely those who had seen the light or combatants, they had been made judges, of sin, who had to give a verdict as well as to execute it. They had full authority, after sins had been confessed, to forgive them or not; both within the power accorded them.

As regards this authority, it was not for them to say anything. The Lord took them just as he found them and gave them this power without leaving them any choice. The choice had been made when they decided to follow the Lord, when they were far from any idea that they would, one day, be endowed with this power. In fact, it meant a complete revolution in their relation with the Lord; it was a conclusion whose premises they had scarcely been able to perceive.

The new power given them was strictly dependent on their receiving the Holy Spirit. Since the disciples were following the Lord, they were desirous of sharing everything that was his. The Holy Spirit was his, and so the charge given them, though unexpected, was logical.

The Lord had no hesitation in giving his apostles such unheard-of power, that of influencing the destiny of the sinner in the most searching way. He did not hesitate, because the power was not given to be exercised according to their personal ability, but according to the ability imparted them by the Spirit. With this power they would always be set between two poles, for they would be under the constant necessity of bringing their understanding of sin into line with their office, itself beyond understanding; they would pass definite human judgments on the gravity of a sin, but all their judgments must be within the setting of their authority. What their own reason suggests to them will not be sufficient, for they must be subject to the reason of the Holy Spirit.

The Lord too, in his life on earth, was never actuated by purely human motives: his acts and decisions arose out of his relationship with the Father in the Holy Spirit. Even when he said: "If it be possible, let this chalice pass from me" (which perhaps reflected his momentary wish), he at once turned to the supernatural will of the Father and desired it to be done. When, therefore, he instituted confession, he made over to the apostles something of his relationship to the Father. He did not first instruct them on this, but, by his action, made them sharers in it, so that, in their dealings with sin, their judgments should have their source in the mystery of the Son's obedience. Often in his earthly life they had seen him do inexplicable things in virtue of an unknown power. He worked signs and wonders that made his relatives think he had taken leave of his senses; and, on those occasions, the apostles did not altogether disagree. Now, however, they were no longer to try to understand by their own power, but by that of the Holy Spirit. Most of all, whenever they should have an opinion, an insight, of their own, they were to discard it for the insight that God gave them, though it remained, on the whole, incomprehensible. From this time, the element beyond understanding is found elsewhere than before; for it is what they themselves bring about by their action, and, in so doing, they experience at a deeper level their union with the Lord. In fact, their experience, in their office as priests, was to extend to the twofold nature of the Son, who is God and man in one Person, an experience that they too, through him, were placed in a situation both one and twofold. From the profound mystery of the Son there came into being a new mystery appropriate to their condition. The double character of their situation, which yet had to be lived as a unity, had the effect in them as of a seed coming up; at times, indeed, they had to be both seed and fruit. Their office, together with the Holy Spirit given them, gave rise to a constant intentness on their part to fruitful action; and this they had to be careful never to let slacken.

On the Mount of Olives they fell asleep. They showed then that, of their own power, they could not remain vigilant, even when expressly admonished by the Lord. This defect meant they could not be present when the whole matter of sin was being dealt with between the Father and the Son. Now, however, that the Lord had spoken and given them this new form of watchfulness – for they must be vigilant, in order to bind and loose – they received it as a gift of the Holy Spirit.

When the Lord promised Peter the keys and made him the rock, Peter could scarcely realize what this gift contained; it was tremendous, obscure. He could see that the Lord had something particular in store for him, but what it was he could not have known at the time. The real content of the promise remained hidden in the future. It was different with the institution of confession. Although the use of the power given still lay in the future, the apostle must have felt how concrete the gift was, however incomprehensible. The fact was clear enough; they were to be able to forgive sins through their receiving the Holy Ghost. They understood that this was to be taken literally, but in their very understanding of the word they were brought up sharply against the incomprehensible. It was the same kind of incomprehensibility that occurs in every Christian life by a sort of refraction, and that, in all the sacraments, makes renewed impact on the believer. The power of forgiving sins is no less incomprehensible than that of changing bread into the Lord's body.

Certainly, the apostles, when they came to celebrate the Supper for the first time, must have trembled at the thought of eating the body of the Lord. Yet the actual changing was wholly dependent on God and on his Word, so that they simply had to perform the act, without any need to understand, to act in pure faith, wholly transparent to the Word. But when they came to bind and loose, they had to understand to some extent, so as to be able to judge; for they had to judge, even if in the Holy Spirit. There the tension was greater between being simply instruments and acting on their own. They were required to serve, but as persons having insight of their own.

Their understanding and will were used as tools for the Spirit's action and in union with him. If the priest hears confessions only as a routine, with divided attention, bored with it all, if he judges sinners on human ethical principles, that shows he has misconceived the mystery of confession; some harm is bound to result. There is a kind of alertness required of the priest, which should prompt a new alertness and vigour in the penitent. The insight he ought to attain, and which makes him share, as a Christian, in the state of his penitent, can only be secured by his own effort. Office and person must be fused in a real unity.

After Easter, the conqueror of sin had the fulness of power which he could impart to the apostles. He had come back to them with a new experience, that of having suffered and died for sinners. The experience of redemption he had acquired in his own person for God and man; and whenever in the future men speak of redemption they speak of him. It was as Redeemer that he gave to his apostles the gift of the Holy Spirit; there is no mention of any request to the Father or any permission from him. He gave them the Spirit entirely on his own, and yet, in so doing, he made over to them a mystery of the Trinity in God; for the Holy Spirit must have been ready and in agreement to be sent by him into his Church. The Son made use of the Spirit for the purpose of the redemption, and the apostles had a share in this power of the Son's, applying it as they saw fit. It was as if the Son, who before his death was the servant of the Father, now wished to make more evident his independent domination; but the independence of a divine Person, when emphasized, often serves to show more clearly the unity of mind and will of all three. The will of the Son is the same as that of the Spirit, and, since the Son's will is always the revelation of the Father's will, the latter is also the will of the Spirit. In what the Son spoke on this occasion, there is no mention of the Father; he was as if hidden in the Son and the Spirit, and yet revealed along with them in the will of both. But what the Father willed to reveal through being thus hidden was the mission of the Son. The Son is not just a servant or instrument; he shares explicitly in the Father's power, communicated to him by the Father without restriction. The disposition made by the Son on this occasion shows clearly that nothing, not even his Passion and death, happened through weakness or limitation. Had the Son said: "I have asked the Father that I may give you the Spirit . . .", he would indeed have been an emissary, but not the eternal Son. When he was on the cross, he handed over all to the Father, even his Spirit, so unreservedly that now it was the Father's will to manifest in all its splendour the power inherent in the Son.

Binding and Loosing

The Son said: "Receive ye the Holy Ghost." He himself had received the Spirit visibly at his baptism; but, before that, the Spirit had received him, to deliver him to his mother on her conceiving him. Everything in God is absolute self-giving, trust, love; each of the three Persons is wholly open to the others. The Son, who became man out of love and desire to give himself, manifested and taught this divine disposition, namely, to be open to the Father in everything, to show him all that goes on in man, not only for the Father to see it, but for him to share it and experience it too. As the Son made all this so manifest, the Father participated in the life of the Son so closely that the Son himself had the experience of this participation and lived by it. Always, whatever the Son said or did found its echo and response in the Father, including the decisive: "Not my will, but thine!", when the Father imposed the mandate for the Passion.

So it is that, in confession, which the Son instituted, the sinner has to show himself to God's representative in self-giving, trust and love; the answer, which decides absolution or its withholding, rests with the confessor. Anyone who, unaware of this connection, should hear only the words about binding and loosing, must find them severe and hard, since the sinner must give himself up unconditionally, whereas the person to whom he does so can, apparently, act with him as he pleases. At best, he must look upon them as an arrangement of justice, since it can well be just to forgive one man, and not another. The Spirit given on that occasion to the apostles must, therefore, be a Spirit of just judgment and reflection. But once it is seen that the life of the Son is one of love, then it becomes evident that these words can only stand for all that his life was, and so be words of love, of supreme love, in fact, since they were the first he uttered after his death of love on the cross. This act of love envisaged, not only each individual, but the Church as a whole. Redemption does not mean that, from then on, each man has the freedom to order his life as he will, and God, finally, sets his approval on the whole in a sort of general absolution. What it does mean is that the redeemed have to enter an institution, the Church, whose form is fixed by God, so as to live there a life pleasing to him. Following the Son has the express meaning of avoiding sin and acceptance of a chastisement that is both an education for life in the Son and penance for sin. The Church-order set up by the Son has its source in his love and is the way to his love, and to this origin and end corresponds the power of binding and loosing.

In the process of education for love, which is itself a preliminary stage of love, there has to be both the possibility of educative discipline (and so of punishment) and the element of penance (also bound up with punishment). There can be no education without authority. And since education is a means, the authority must be enabled to judge the state of the person in question, and what is better for him as an individual to attain the love aimed at, whether binding or loosing. For instance, anyone who fails to perceive the essence of sin as absence of love, must be educated to see it. This could be done by making him continue to bear a particular burden, till he realizes it really is a burden. All penitents know of this possibility necessarily imposed by loving authority; and if on account of confessional secrecy, they generally do not know who has had his sins retained, it is enough that they know of the possibility in itself. It is like the Church's treasury of prayer, the existence of which is known to the faithful, though they cannot say who benefits from it and in what way. They know that there are persons in the Church whom she chooses for this discipline, whether or not these men feel the means appointed to be justified or onerous; they will never be those who have completely turned away, because they have once openly exerted themselves for liberation from sin. They know also that there are others who, from love, do all they can to receive absolution. In this way there is communion in prayer between those whose sins have been remitted and those whose sins have been retained.

The believer has no doubt, as regards the treasury of prayer, that he can take from it and also add to it. If, however, he is one of those "loosed" from sin, and knows that there are those who are "bound", he can, conscious of his communion with them, suffer along with them, atone for them, and even, in a certain way, insert them into his confession. There is, indeed, no single sacrament in the Church that is wholly private; they are all means and occasions for unity. Each of them binds together all believers that have any connection with the sacrament, whether they directly receive it or not. The sacraments are among the most powerful forces of unity, for they act in a most mysterious way to lead Christians to the unity of the Church. This unity does not only consist in a community and harmony of outlook, taste, mode of life. All this can, indeed, be the expression of unity, and the sacraments communicate this form of unity too; but the real, essential unity is not there, and it is into that unity that the sacraments incorporate men. The unity of the Church is, essentially, love, and those who are sacramentally incorporated and led into this love, receive the sacraments, including confession, with a sense of the communion of saints. If a person is still "bound", he is for that very reason, on the way to love; and those who are "loosed" are thereby enabled to be conscious of their union with the "bound", and to conduct themselves accordingly.

In the course of his earthly life, the Lord in part bound, in part loosed, the sins he encountered; bound in the case of the Jews, loosed in that of the disciples and of the penitent women. Nevertheless, he bore all sins and made reparation for them. It is self-evident that he could not remit the sins of those who did not believe in him, such as the Jews; they, indeed, wanted nothing from him. Nothing was further from their minds than to make confession to him, to imitate his attitude of openness before the Father. But there are also those who desired to confess and open their souls, but do not obtain absolution. They make their confession, are contrite, yet they do not receive absolution. What is the explanation? Are they, perhaps, the victims of some priestly whim? Have they penance to bear for others? Or is it in the nature of certain sins that those who commit them know they do something unforgiveable?

In that case, there would be, perhaps, a division between sins, not only between mortal and venial, but between forgiveable and unforgiveable, between the sin against the Holy Ghost and those not explicitly such. But that would lead to quite untenable conclusions, and so there must be another explanation why confession may not suffice for absolution even when made with sincerity. The element lacking must be looked for in contrition, which seems sufficient to the penitent, but not to the confessor. The penitent has the will to avoid the sin, but not the proximate occasion of it; or he fails to see the gravity of the sin which the confessor retains; or he thinks he can master a certain situation, but does not see what scandal it could cause. There is always some reservation or other that the penitent ought not to have; his disposition falls short of what is needed. He is caught up in a misconception, taking confession for something other than it really is, namely absolute submission to God's word in order to reproduce the disposition of the Son before the Father.

Judas lived, like the other apostles, in the company of the Lord. Though he had not the Holy Spirit, he did not, perhaps, seem essentially different from the rest. His sins, however, were retained, because his life in the Lord's company was not a following of him, not submission and obedience, not confession. He had already found, and no longer sought; his finding kept him from seeking further.

In the Church the topmost rank is occupied by those of real holiness, the middle by sinners who have received absolution, the lowest by those whose sins are retained, whose absolution has to be deferred. Outside the Church are those who do not confess at all.

The Lord, being God, means by his words always more than we can grasp, and some of this meaning is disclosed at each fresh encounter with him. We can never look on any one encounter as complete and done with, meaning one thing and nothing beyond. It would be essentially unchristian to hold that we could fix the essence of, say, a Holy Communion in a number of definitions or a summation of many different aspects. There will always be some element of the Lord's action, being, mystery that transcends these. The mystery of communion with him is enshrined in him, not in us. It is just the same with confession. We know what we have to do, when we go to confession; we distinguish the individual acts, examination of conscience, contrition and resolution, confession and absolution. We know that we desire peace with the Lord. But the mystery of the disposition which constitutes a good confession lies in the grace of the Lord, not in us. We can never survey our disposition so as to be able to say of it that it is good, it is adequate. The Holy Spirit, however, endows the confessor with the grace to discern whether our basic disposition is sufficient or not. If absolution be given, we may accept in obedience the presence of a sufficient disposition, though, along with this, there is also an awareness of our insufficiency, since we know, just because we confess and are contrite, that we are never what the all-holy will of God would have us be. The blessedness of the purity bestowed on us by the absolution is, as it were, held suspended in the wretchedness of our feeling that we always somehow fall short. But if our sins are not remitted, it is no longer a vague feeling of inadequacy we have but a certain knowledge presented to our spirit so starkly as to stir and shake our whole being as Christians to the very depths. It may be that we see immediately where we fall short. More likely, even if we are told where, whether in contrition, resolution, sense of sin, and so on, what will happen is that we will see, for the first time, the immense abyss of our inadequacy, once the mask is torn away from our complacency. For we tried to find our sufficiency, not in the infinite love of God, but in ourselves. We went to confession with the idea that we knew the drill, and so degraded the mystery to a kind of automatic process of cleansing; but grace was absent, since we did not wish to submit to the law of grace. Once we realize our inadequacy was far more than we suspected, we begin to discover, with grace, the boundless resources of the divine Master.

The Life of Christ as Preparatory to the Institution

CHILDHOOD:

The early years of Christ's life were his initiation into life as a man and into his mission, but also an initiation of those near him into a relationship with God like his own. His mother's "fiat" expressed her total preparedness, and of Joseph we learn that, after the angel's appearance in the dream, he realized the way appointed in regard to Christ and followed it. One might, at first, think that the appearances of the angel to Mary and Joseph might, through their strong impact, have elicited just an isolated act of assent, whose consequences for their whole life were not clearly envisaged. If each of them, at the moment of the vision or just after, had been asked how they expected to prove their fidelity, they might have felt confused; possibly they would have said that God always provides the help and means for the purposes he has in view. Now this help, this means, is there expressly in the Son. His whole life long that is what he will be for them, but more particularly in his childhood; he is the source for his parents of the strength to remain faithfully in the way of God. As yet he propounds no doctrine, calls no disciples, keeps his relationship with the Father concealed within himself, but the disposition corresponding to all this cannot be hidden; and inasmuch as it necessarily shows itself, he imparts it to them.

This disposition is one of absolute openness, the attitude of confession, which he presents to Mary and Joseph as his constant attitude through life. They look to him in their most momentous decisions, such as the flight into Egypt; they look to him too in all the small things of life. They foster and cherish him, and, in their continuous association with him, become practised in the disposition which is his.

For Mary, the Immaculate Virgin, it was not difficult to imitate him in this. We might say even that it was "child's play", a particularly appropriate effect of the child's action on her. Joseph too was a holy man, who, in his constant association with mother and child, entered almost with ease into the disposition characteristic of the New Covenant. Mary was redeemed in advance and destined to receive this child in order to be initiated by him into the mysteries of God. Joseph, however, was destined from all time to be the husband of the virgin and to make her and her child the focus both of his outward concern and inward occupation. But all this originates in the child and comes from him. What he will be later and how he will act is already shown in childish form; rather as it might be said of a great architect that, even as a child, he built wonderful things with his wooden blocks.

Binding and loosing presuppose that one knows the commandments, is well versed in doctrine and capable of living accordingly. When the child of twelve taught in the temple and explained the doctrine of his Father, that was all part of the preparation for confession. It served to spread the knowledge of the Father, and that would give men a deeper insight into their own sinfulness. The doctors of the law saw how the divine law should be interpreted and applied, saw too what knowledge the child already possessed, who would later expound his own doctrine with supreme authority. Not yet did he let himself be known as the Messias. What, however, was clear was that there was one among the people who was obviously taught by God himself in view of a future mission.

Those of his hearers who were converted would, perhaps, later come to play a particular part in the understanding of the Son's self-confession. The individual confession is a preliminary exercise in sharing the confession of Christ. These men would, perhaps, be able to provide the people with a true explanation and understanding of things which the Lord only indicated in outline. The child's temple discourse is itself, essentially, a clarification of how sin looks from the standpoint of the New Covenant, and how it is to be treated. The Son went to the temple as someone of learning, in order to instruct the learned; just as he lived in Joseph's house as a believer, to show forth the belief he had as a child. As long as he was a child, he was spared conflict with evil; the doctors were astonished to hear how he spoke, they asked him questions, but did not dispute with him. As a man, the Lord was to preach in a more apostolic, controversial fashion. The child of twelve propounded the teaching of the New Covenant in a way that seemed to the Jews pertinent and acceptable, indicating all that was contained in the law of the Father, and clarifying the doctrine of the Old Covenant while, at the same time, showing all its profundity.

ENTRANCE ON THE PUBLIC LIFE:

At home the Son lived in a narrow circle of people who believed in him from the beginning and so gave him a spiritual home. The child found a home where not only was he, as it were, "brought up", but received honour and love, and this allowed the full development of all that lay in him. The love he found stirred him to a life of action, and this life, in turn, acted on that love. Consequently, when, through the Baptist's action, a wider sphere was opened up to him, he was bound to love all he encountered there in the way he loved those in the narrower sphere, that is with the Father always in view. Yet now the question arose what his manner of life ought to be if it was to manifest this love effectively to the aloof and uninitiated. From his own attitude of confession there slowly emerged the idea of instituting confession, and the question how he could communicate to them his own love. The institution was, in the end, the fruit of his Passion and death, but it was equally the completion and crowning of all he strove for throughout his life.

At home in Nazareth the questions were limited by the number of people there, and his intercourse with Joseph and Mary served as a training for his later contact with the crowds. In the case of those few, the disposition, the starting-point, was right, and only needed broadening. In the case of the many, however, a change was needed from the outset. He saw all the invincible obstacles, conscious and unconscious, their estrangement, of which the causes were different for each person. Though confession afterwards seems to follow a uniform pattern, it has nevertheless grown out of the Lord's innumerable individual experiences; consequently, it thus conceals the possibility of being something different and special to each, corresponding to his own situation, and yet capable of bringing each one closer to the Father.

Certainly, one way that could have been adopted was for the Son to make known to men his own contemplation of the Father, presenting it in so attractive a form as to draw them to imitate it. He could have been a sort of theorist or mystic of divine truth, but, in his public life, he always broke through his contemplation and theory into the practical sphere, carried his vision of the Father into the apostolate among men. Those who live solely on the plane of speculation are liable not to see in their neighbour someone to be loved in a practical, effective way. The Son, in his life among men, was always asking himself what he could do to make the mysteries of the love of the Trinity accessible to men. The effective means is not only teaching or knowledge, but, above all, the sacraments, and, in particular, confession.

When God spoke to Adam, it was, at first, to a creature who was entirely open before him. Later, he spoke to a creative alienated from him, and to him he showed, in that he continued to make himself heard, that he was stronger than both Adam and the serpent together. He showed his supreme power as a prelude to any further development, the force of his voice when he once deigned to speak. This force was not something Adam had, an overwhelming desire to hear the word. On the contrary, it was Adam who was overwhelmed by it, in his flight from the voice of God. He was humiliated in being obliged, in spite of all, to hear what God said to him. Now, however, the Son takes on himself some of this humiliation, suffering for all that each of them might be given a kind of willingness to speak with God in confession, to let himself be purified and changed through God's word. Each time the Son met with a sinner, he took on himself something of this humiliation. Nor did he do so exclusively for his contemporaries. His will was to redeem all men, and so he bore, on the cross, every kind of humiliation, and, afterwards, opened to all sinners, in instituting confession, the way to God. Both these acts of his were the outcome of what he experienced in his commerce with sinners.

Only God can effectively bear the world's sin, and when the Son took it on himself as man, that is the positive sign that God is turning to estranged man, hastens after man in flight from him. 'I know that you flee from me', says God, 'but know that I am ready to receive you. However gravely you have sinned, never believe that I have abandoned you. Always you have the way open to me. Never doubt the presence of God; in the Church, in the Eucharist, God has set up a reminder that he is there, and has ordained the step you must take to reach him: confession.' It was to create this openness in man that the Son drew humiliation on himself, and laid it on himself, who indeed was God. The step man must take is already given in the grace offered. The very existence of such a step is itself a grace, and yet, when a man takes it, the merit is his. Through grace man has received the genuine possibility of returning to God: and the way of grace, prepared by God, has a twofold aspect, being invisible in God and visible in the world, invisible in Christ's divinity, visible in his humanity and in his Church. He took on himself man's abasement and suffered it to the point of death and the cross, but opened a way of following him in suffering, a way of return in grace through confession and absolution.

He suffered because men turned their backs on God and would not confess their sins. His suffering from sins unacknowledged and unspecified merited, in the first place, the gift to be able to confess them. The sin whose burden he bore on the cross was the sum of all unspoken, evaded confessions; and he bore it as man, but in the will of the Triune God to take the burden from men. Otherwise, his bearing it would have been incomprehensible and purposeless. In doing so, in suffering as God and man, he opened up a new way on which man could encounter God. As the Son of God, he knew he was at one with the Father's will, and that God approved of what he did. When one of the just men of the Old Testament suffered, he saw in it a kind of just punishment, but the question of expiation remained unclarified; and since the Jews had no knowledge of eternal life, all took place on the earthly plane, where the relationship between sin and expiation can never be clearly discerned. Man may, indeed, believe, may be orientated to God, may desire to show him his condition, may even experience guidance from God: but so long as access to eternal life has not been given, real confession is not possible. Only on the cross was the barrier broken, for then God's relationship to man was not merely that of heaven's ruler, who can work miracles and speak with the sons of men, but of one whose heaven man could enter together with the Son, since his death on the cross had built the bridge into eternal life. The Son is the way, and in confession he sets the sinner on that way. So completely is he the way and the door that the very act of opening oneself and turning to the Father is to enter on eternal life, means separation from one's own sins, communion with all who confess, and gives a new power to hear, in the Holy Spirit, the voice of the Father. In a sense, confession is a mirror of the cross, wherein, however, all the elements have become, through the Son's atoning act, so light and easy that only faith can perceive the real likeness.

When the Lord left Nazareth, he lost the physical and spiritual protection of his own land, and entered the region dominated by the cross. He looked on his body and soul as the instrument on which his whole Passion would be performed, culminating in death, an infinitely manifold symphony to be given final unity in the sacrament of penance. This sacrament directly recalls all the mysteries, which began with the active life, when the Son, visible as man, started to take up the burden of the world's sins. The thousand occurrences of his life on earth had, as their final result, the completion and rounding-off of this sacrament.

THE MIRACLES:

When the Lord worked a miracle, it was in view of the effect on men; he saw its ability to engender faith and keep it in vigour. Through each new miracle more men come to him, or the faith of those already converted is strengthened; and, in addition, there is a wider circle of persons inquiring, influenced, interested, to whom it opens up a new approach. In the miracles, too, "power went out from him" so that they continued to work their effect. And, since each work of the Son involved the Father and the Holy Spirit, it comprised a certain trinitarian element. The object, however, of the miracles was to free men from sin and bring them to faith.

After the Passion Christ knew that his return to the Father was imminent, that, after the Ascension, he would no longer, as a man on earth, work miracles that caused power to go out of him. But, at the same time, he knew that, on the cross, he had given up all power, so that he died weak and helpless. He, therefore, instituted confession, which would draw on all the power of his life that he had foregone, and, in its constant practice, would be always renewing the effectiveness of the miracles he worked on earth. Confession, in fact, is his enduring miracle given to the Church, and in it all his former miracles are contained, visibly and efficaciously.

Confession as a miracle, is, primarily, an event; it is the great transformation of sinner into saint, and so it introduces the act of redemption into the individual life. The Eucharist is the gift and communication of a permanent presence of the Lord, while confession gives participation in what took place on the cross, in the absolution of the earth brought about by heaven. The Eucharist, is more of a pure gift; while confession consists of man's own acts of turning to God, contrition and confession of sins. At the Last Supper, the whole situation was dominated by the Lord, his action, the commission he gave, his words; and the Eucharist always has this character. In confession, the fact of sin is so central that man together with his situation, past and present, is summoned to co-operate with the Lord.

So it was that, in the miracles too – examples are the cures of the deaf and dumb man, of the blind, the dropsical man, of the man possessed with a devil, of the woman with a haemorrhage – man was considered in his particular state and given what it required. Invariably it was a case of something lacking, of someone sick and hungry in body or in soul. The miracle made this situation one which applied to the Lord himself, who took it over, made himself responsible, and brought healing. He sought out starving man where he lay. Now that he has gone to heaven, man must show himself to go to him, but the Lord has already said where and how he is to be found. Each man, in his sinfulness, has to face his own state of want, but, at the same time, to see that it can be remedied through a miracle of the Lord.

CHRIST'S PREACHING:

Christ, in his preaching, glorified the Father, bringing men to the knowledge of him so that they would be stirred up to glorify the Father in their turn; but he never forgot the purpose of his mission, which was to glorify him through redemption. Every word he spoke can be considered in this aspect. Everything he said about love, about the Father, most of his parables too, had a connection with the sinner's meeting with God to which he later gave the form of confession. Men had of their own accord turned their backs on God; and so, equally of their own volition, they had to take the way back, or, at least, make some movement of return.

In this there is something resembling the Incarnation, in that the Son too offered himself, of his own accord, to the Father, and advanced to this work of redemption in perfect freedom, of which all that he spoke bore the stamp. His whole course from the Father and back to him clearly expresses his freedom of will and, at the same time, the unfailing certainty with which he pursued this way and carved it out for us. In his preaching, he aimed at imparting to men this same freedom and certainty; whether he spoke in parables or proverbs, or taught and instructed his apostles, always he pointed out the way. The way he followed in freedom was a pattern for those who had voluntarily turned from the Father, and voluntarily—through grace—must return to him. Indeed, the Son, in sinlessly leaving the Father, had taken on himself something akin to sin, namely the element of estrangement from God that lay in the Incarnation and reached its culmination on the cross. His cry of dereliction could equally well have been the cry of a sinner who can see no possible way of escape. He himself had sold everything to buy for the Father the pearl of redeemed man; and man must follow him by selling all to return to the Father.

As his life advanced, he took the world's sin on himself more and more. This action of his, however, would have remained unnoticed by men, unless his teaching broadened out, at the same time, to a universal doctrine, valid for all times and peoples. If we were to contemplate his cross, while ignorant of his teaching, we could easily gain the impression of onesidedness, of a certain fanaticism. But when he made known his own being and his way in all its various directions, while preserving its unity in this multiplicity, or showing its unity through this very multiplicity, then it was that the meaning of the cross became evident, though still not in its entirety. For in fact all his utterances, all his parables, lead in the end to the cross; and, likewise, the confession of each man, however personal its form, expresses the unity of the sacrament, which, in its turn, expresses the one redemption on the cross. It is the personal gift of redemption made once and for all to each individual in the way in which he can receive and apply it. For this reason, confession, in all the different forms it takes, works powerfully to form the communion of saints. Each confession, each individual disposition thereto, complements all the others, not only because all sins are interconnected, but, more essentially, because all confessions of sin are gathered together in the Lord and his sacrament, and from this unity derive their efficacy.

There is, consequently, an imperative necessity for the Lord to speak to us, arising from his will to redeem us. He cannot, however, just speak, without ever receiving an answer. Nor can we, henceforth, rely solely on the Father making up for all our failures, for it is the Lord's will to have us as his brethren and fellow-workers. But we can only make answer, if we are without sin; and so the Lord chooses to speak to us at the times when he has purified us from sin, when we are able to hear him and speak to him. So, for example, he speaks words of decisive import, when he has worked some miracle of body or soul. The Father then sees in the subject of the miracle the Son's purity from sin with which he is really endowed. That is why the Son instituted confession, a continuously repeated miracle of purification, so as, through his priest, to enter on a real dialogue with us. The acts of contrition and confession, the counsels of the confessor, are words spoken according to the mind and will of the Lord, and which are worthy of the Father's hearing. In them the sinner achieves detachment from self, not only for that moment, but in such a way that the grace of the Lord pours into him and purifies his inmost being. The Father sees what belongs to the Son going out into the penitent. And, with this penetration by grace there comes also the word of the Lord, itself a form of his grace. All his words have to do with the process of confession; they all belong to the single act in which he redeemed us, redeemed the whole world. Even if we fail to hear some of his words, if we do not understand and grasp them all, there yet, with his grace, penetrates into us something of his own being as Word; every grace being his is a grace of the eternal Word, and empowers us anew to speak with God. On that account, each of his words acts on the hearer to purify him, for each is grace and redemption.

The Sermon on the Mount, the final discourse of Christ, each of his utterances has the power to create in the hearer purity from sin and preparedness for God, but for this confession to the Lord is necessary. Whoever desires to abide in the word of the Lord must make confession to him. No one can marvel at the word of God and reverence it, and, at the same time, remain shut up in his own heart. He must submit himself to the command of confession, to the office of binding and loosing. That is the will of the Word that gave the Holy Spirit to the apostles. Only those who confess their sins to the Church's authority have access to the full meaning of the word; otherwise, it is understood merely philologically and in an eclectic manner. The word of God must be taken and understood in the setting where it both purifies and enlightens, acts both as sermon and as sacrament.

The word taken merely as instruction is a preliminary to the total word, the word that redeems. If the Lord had not founded the Church as his bride, the word of the gospel would have been his greatest gift to man. Now, however, behind his word, his command of love, there stands himself, whom we have to recognize in our neighbour, not only symbolically, but literally. His word and command, therefore, presuppose the transforming and redeeming power of his grace. They presuppose, too, the Church as his mystical body, and, equally, the Church in its hierarchical office. His word is the divine fulness of power given him by the Father to administer, with which he has invested the Church for the ends of love.

All this may be stated in a different way and more profoundly. The Son lives in uninterrupted union with the Father, in virtue of which he knows that he always recognizes the Father's will and does it. The union of the believer with the Church's authority is an image, given him by the Son, of this union with the Father; for just as the Son, being God and man, is, in virtue of this union, always open to the Father, so the Christian, through his openness to the authority of the Church, is united to Christ and, with him, to the Trinity. The Son, being open to the Father and to the world, is the Word confessing, and this pre-eminently on the cross, in his great confession of the world's sins. And we, in confessing our sins in the setting of the Church, receive a share in the Lord's nature as Word. Preaching and confession are related to each other as the Lord's life and his cross, and, in a still more universal sense, as his heavenly and earthly life, inasmuch as the latter was, as a whole, determined by the law of sin.

THE PASSION:

The risen Christ owed the apostles, in all their joy at seeing him, an explanation why he had died and was once more alive, why he had utterly failed and yet conquered, why he had suffered and was now rejoicing, why he had left them and was back among them. On all these counts he vindicated himself in instituting confession, as if his whole life, his acts and death, were sufficiently explained by this concluding word; as if the apostles needed nothing further to be equipped for their mission. There was no question to be put to the Lord, no request for explanation, which was not already answered, not already anticipated, by his words of institution. Before the Passion, he had spoken much of the cross to come, and given the puzzled apostles many opportunities to reach an understanding. All these prophecies, however, concerned only the individual in question; the Son of man must be delivered up and suffer these things; and the apostles saw in them, at the most, only the exterior aspect. But the words of institution illuminated the Passion from within, revealed its central meaning and purpose, so central that the faith of the apostles was required for the disclosure of the inner connection between the Passion and confession. The Lord did not speak again expressly of the Passion, yet the words of institution point back to it unquestionably and cannot be explained apart from it. Conversely, too, the Passion can only be explained through these words. It is from the standpoint of confession that the apostles were to contemplate and understand the Son's death and resurrection, his whole destiny.

Now they understood as well that the Lord had taken them up with him into his Passion, both those who were actually present and all the others who only knew about it. These he had taken up in that he bore their sins also. The apostles saw in him so wonderfully transformed the living proof that they too were changed. Yet the whole explanation did not lie in this, but in the words of institution, which summoned them, not only to realize what had happened with the Lord and with them, but to enact it themselves. They only understood the eternal life they had received through the Passion and resurrection by communicating it to others. The apostles came to understand death and resurrection in their administration of the sacrament of penance. The man, however, who performs the act knows what it means; and the Lord taking the apostles into his Passion, knew what he was doing; he was acting in union with the Father and associating them with him. But when he gave them authority for confession, then they knew that they had been, in the Father's eyes, joined with him in what he had done, not indeed by their own merit and understanding, but because he had so acted and they were present.

From Easter to Pentecost

The Lord, when he instituted confession, saw each particular phase of it, its initial phase, its subsequent development, and its end in the return of man, purified from sin, to God and to his mission in the world. For the Lord himself this return to God and assumption of world-dominion took place in the Ascension.

Seen from the standpoint of confession, the forty days between Easter and the Ascension were a time of suspension, as when the words of absolution still re-echo before the life of grace has been received again; or like a pause between the conclusion of the earthly mission and the assumption of the mission of the Incarnate Lord in heaven. It was a time free of any sort of oppressiveness, when he knew he had done the will of the Father to the very end, had realized the highest possible achievement for any man on earth. At Easter the fulness of the Father's absolution was imparted to the Son. He was like someone who, after receiving absolution, remains on his knees overwhelmed by grace, not yet rising to leave the church and resume his ordinary work. It was the end of confession, which, for the Son, was expressed in his Ascension, his return to the Father.

If everything ended with this return, the Christian would indeed have received absolution from sin, but would know nothing further. He would have lost his bearings, being relieved of his burden without knowing what he should do with his new strength. For that reason, both for the Lord and for the believer, Ascension leads straight into Pentecost. When the Son sent his own and the Father's Spirit into the world, then there began his own dominion over the world and, for his apostles now redeemed, their Christian mission in the world. Absolution is not an end, but a new beginning. The Lord does not abandon those purified from sin, but visits them anew in sending them his Spirit. What looks like a conclusion is, in reality, a starting-point; for the apostles, the beginning of hearing confession. As long as he remained with them, there was no occasion to confess sins to anyone but the Lord; but now there began his life in the mystical and hierarchical Church.

The Spirit and the Church belong together. When the Son revealed himself on earth, it was for a double purpose, pointing back to the Father and the Spirit and forward to the future communion of saints. He is essentially a mediator, always pointing beyond himself. And nowhere does he bind together the two ends, the Spirit and the Church, more indissolubly than in confession, where two men meet, one as repentant sinner, the other as charged by the Spirit to remit sin. It is on this way, formed and trodden by the Lord himself, that man comes to the Father; and the Spirit of the way, which is Christ, and the Spirit of the end, which is the Father, is one and the same.

5. THE CHURCH AND CONFESSION

Bride and Confession

THE WORK of the Church, as the bride of Christ, is to prepare herself for the bridegroom. She has no need to question her worthiness, for she knows that the Lord has given her for her adornment all that this perfection requires. Then, when he returned to the Father, apparently withdrawing from her in order to make her see her real greatness and, at the same time, testing her, she realized how much he had given into her charge. As bride, she now possessed the administration of his concerns on earth and responsibility for them; and, when this time comes to an end, she will have to give account of her stewardship.

She has understood the Lord's aim; the love at work, the love which formed her, the love which was to be communicated to men. In each Christian she sees something of her own being, sees him as a mirror of herself. For that reason, she endeavours to form each one according to the Lord's expectation, exhorting him, impressing that stamp upon him, so that the image, which she herself is, may be reproduced ever more visibly in the world.

When the Church, as instructed by the Lord, brings her children to confession, she wishes to make her own bridal quality shine out in each of her members as it does in her. She knows, indeed, that she cannot form all her children to be perfectly holy. Yet, just as the Lord made exacting demands on her, so she asks the utmost of her members, that they may attain the greatest possible purity. She also knows that the truly pure are actively impelled to transmit this purity to others, in the Church's name, to stir men up to greater purity. This driving force works by example and intercession that bears men along in its sweep and makes their love more ardent.

The image of the Lord is present in each individual soul, and, therefore, the Church, in the commands she gives, invades the inmost recesses of the soul. She addresses her warnings and demands to all her members, including those who are lukewarm and estranged from her. For the sinner, she fixes the minimum of Easter confession; for the saint she prescribes a particular quality of confession, which she believes is something owed to the whole community.

The Church is concerned that each one, humbled and raised up through confession, should feel he belongs to the communion of saints and is newly taken up into it in order to discharge some responsible function in the Church. Confession is a sacrament that pertains primarily to the Church, so that the individual should not consider his own conscience as the supreme arbiter; his sins and purification from them are not just a private matter between him and God. The Church plays a decisive part as mediator, having been given the mediatorial office of Christ. She has to give account of all who are numbered among her members.

Everyone, not only the priest, has a responsible function in the Church. A good Christian in contact with a member of the Church who is a habitual sinner is concerned that he should go to confession. The priest too has a duty arising not only from

Christ's commission, but from all who are concerned in the matter, to take on the responsibilities of a confessor, even though this commission from the laity is not explicit; for anyone who is aware of Christ's love within him knows it has demands to make. Confession, therefore, is not just a private matter for the individual, nor something solely between him and the priest. Each one confesses as a member of the community of penitents, in order to enter anew the communion of saints. In confessing, he never ceases for a moment to be a member of the community, just as the Son always belonged to the Trinity, even when he, and he alone, was man. None of his actions is comprehensible by itself, apart from his unity of life with the Father in the Spirit; none without reference to his love and responsibility to the "divine community". Something of his mission, of his awareness of the most exacting demands and responsibility laid on him, the Lord has imparted to his Church, both as an official body and as the communion of saints. He himself did not come only to live as a model for others. His mission was apostolic, to draw others along with him, and they should all feel themselves to be one community.

The Church has received the Spirit and mind of Christ. When she makes extreme claims on the individual by breaking in on his private, personal sphere, she is only doing what she has seen the Lord doing and learned from him. The best of the Church's possessions consist in what she has directly received from the Lord and, in obedience to him, communicates to her members. The power and authority she uses in dispensing the sacraments are a sign of her authenticity and vitality. It is a power containing a promise of great grace to be fulfilled in those who feel the impact of her living force and assent to it. The only bad thing would be for the Church, in dispensing the means of grace, to adapt herself to the mediocre, for a lukewarm penitent to meet with a lax confessor and so to feel nothing of what happened at the institution of the sacrament. For in that event alone, in the personal relationship of the bridegroom to the bride, can be understood what a sacrament is and is meant to be; and each, as a new contact of Christ with the Church, reveals his relationship with the Father. A sacrament must not be looked on as a mere arrangement or as an established procedure: its institution by Christ must ever be borne in mind.

The penitent easily forgets that he is a member of the community and performs a communal act. He thinks he has to establish right order within himself and for his own sake. The Church, however, does not forget his member function. Often, it is not so much grave sin going unconfessed as the general slackness of a life without confession, the general lack of direction and fervour, that has its effect on the community. People become complacent, narrow and self-centred, and decline to follow the Church's guidance. They may, perhaps, regard a particular practice of the Church to be intolerable. It can, indeed, happen that the utterances of the Church or of some of her representatives sound dated and stale, because the true word that proceeds from the word of the Lord is no longer living and effectual in them. We have learnt to accomodate ourselves to mediocrity in religion and to expect it in advance; we fail to realize that the word of God can bring about a radical change in men. But if the Church no longer believes in the power of the word, how is the individual to hear the word of God sounding through her utterances? The Church, when she hears anyone's confession, should detect in it the sound of her own confession to the Lord. In the absolution she imparts, she should herself receive absolution; she should participate to such a degree in the hearing of what is confessed, in the absolution given, in the binding and loosing, that in all that concerns the individual she should be aware of being likewise affected. For this reason, she should bring it home to the individual penitent that he is not alone; that precisely in and through the sacrament he is a member of the Church. But then the Church receiving the confession must, of course, look on the penitent as a part of herself. Through the Lord she is enabled to distribute the gift of his grace, but, in doing so, should feel as much joy as those who receive, greater in fact, since it is more blessed to give. Like the Mass, confession is, for confessor and penitent, priest and layman, a meal in common.

Confession in Relation to the other Sacraments

The Incarnate Son differed from other men in being without sin. Ignorant of his miracles, oblivious of his discourses, one could still have inferred his divine mission from his sinlessness. He lived among sinners as their redeemer, and saw how much sin had estranged them from the Father. He wanted to catch hold of man fallen from the way, give him a secure hold, throw him the anchor of grace, set up signposts to show the way back to God. The sacraments are the means whereby he lays hold of men.

As long as he was on the earth, he could direct men to them by his own words; he baptized or had them baptized, promised and gave his flesh and blood, provided for the anointing of the sick, sent down the Holy Spirit on the Church. He knew, however, that, after he had gone, the objection would be raised that men were too much estranged from God to be able to use these means. He, therefore, instituted a sacrament for the exclusive use of sinners, which would take hold of men from below and raise them, seize them in their state of guilt and alienation. No one can say that estrangement from God did not weigh heavily on men, and that it would not be good for them to be rid of this burden. The Son, who lives without sin and any kind of concealment in the presence of the Father, knows what is good for man. The sinner lives more or less in a condition of sin; he does not really believe that he can break with sin, but feels the burden of it, and longs, at least at times, to do away with it. The sacrament of penance is the constantly renewed moment of purification, which, if a person's faith is strong and active, is capable of spreading itself over whole tracts of his life. It makes him approximate more to the purity of the Lord, both in act and, increasingly, as a habitual state.

The sacrament of penance takes hold of the sinner in his estrangement from God. All the sacraments do so in their own way, and so reveal a part of the nature of the Church, as a means to bring about man's conversion. Confession, however, effects this in a special degree, and is therefore an exceptionally clear sign of what the Church is. It gives visible form to the fact that the Church exists for all sinners. Communion, on the other hand, which is for those purified from sin, would be, by itself, too exclusive, too terrifying, for sinners. I, as a sinner, know that I disfigure the "communion of saints". I have been baptized, but I do not live accordingly; confirmed, but I am no apostle of Christ. I go to Mass, but it means nothing to me; the sermon is either too profound or too commonplace, it says nothing to me. I am aware of all the efforts the Church makes on my account, how she exhorts, consoles, warns me, but all to no purpose. I have known myself for a long time now, what I can and cannot do. The example of the saints is proposed to me, but I am not one of them. I live in sin, and, as a sinner, I always have the last word in regard to the Church.... But when I am told that the confessional is the place set apart for sinners, it is clear at once that that is the place for me. It was intended, in fact, for me, made just for my needs. Of course, I can still find something to complain about confession, but that does not mean I do not know that it answers the needs of my present situation. If anyone talks about the communion of saints, I know quite well I do not belong to it. But if someone says: There is a communion of sinners, who belongs to it?, I know for certain that I do.

The nature of confession gives me some insight into the life of the Church. When I am taken as a sinner and set free from my sins, I know that I am readmitted; I was taken as an individual, but, through confession, restored to the community of the Church. While I was making my confession, I may have felt quite solitary and separate, but I was so only in appearance. In reality, I was there in the community of penitents, and, whatever the differences in the various sacramental communities, they have one thing in common, that they form part of the community of the Church. Each member, as he returns, realizes that he was always a child of this community, even when his sins prevented him feeling it and weakened the bond that joined him; he sees that the Church had a claim on him in virtue of his baptism.

Confession means being brought back to the centre. Whether I was far off or not, whether my attachment to sin is finally destroyed or only weakened, I am taken back by the firm hand of the Church, which walks along with each believer so that he may not fall into the abyss. And anyone who has the least inkling of this grace knows how ignoble, how ungrateful it would be to turn back to sin in the knowledge of being able to confess again.

When I have confessed and so realized how perfectly this

source of grace meets my needs, the value of all the other sacraments is suddenly brought home to me. Confession used to seem to me like a life-belt thrown out from the Church, something specially adapted for sinners. But it is, as such, a sacrament, like all the others and inseparable from them. To view it in isolation would be as unreasonable as to take the Lord's words, by which he instituted it, in isolation from all the rest of his words. Through confession, which is always something experienced vitally, the other sacraments acquire new significance, especially baptism and confirmation, which had communicated to the penitent a new purity. Those who have confessed realize that they have received something bought for them by the Lord in his Passion, something pertaining to Christ. They are reminded that they were given, at baptism, a sign of their belonging to Christ, and that sin had obscured it. Now, however, through confession, their baptismal innocence is restored to its splendour. Baptism, which can only be received once, imprints an indelible character; it is like a perennial plant covered up in winter that blossoms anew each spring. Confession reactivates the grace of baptism, and also each new confession revitalizes the grace of earlier ones; just as fresh sins reanimate earlier sins. Someone who has fallen into sin more less inadvertently and, after being told in confession the gravity of the sin, falls again and again, may incur an increasing measure of guilt. And it is a mystery of divine love that each new grace bears traces of previous graces, previous absolutions, joining up with and reinforcing them.

The reviviscence of the grace of confirmation chiefly depends on the purpose of amendment in confession. Contrition leads the penitent to resolve to sin more. For this he needs a special power; but in the strengthening of faith that confirmation brings, there is given the Christian a gift of perseverance that is afterwards obscured by sin and so falls into oblivion. The Christian life derives its power of endurance chiefly from the sacraments. Parts of it, like a garment, are torn by sin, and mended by confession so well that no "mend" is to be seen and the original state of wholeness is restored. But just as the soul is an integral whole, so are all the sacraments together. One always bears some reference to the others; in each all the rest are offered. It is as if someone were wet through, and the person drying him were to say: 'You have your raincoat, your umbrella; why don't you use them?' The Christian is constantly brought to see, through the way all the sacraments are connected, with how much care and foresight he is surrounded.

Communion was instituted before the Passion, but the Mass was only completed in the Passion and only available for the Church from Easter. The Last Supper, then, was a promise, whereas confession was, at Easter, immediate fulfilment. At the Supper, the Lord brought his disciples into the centre of the Church characterized by the presence of Judas and the prospect of the Passion; at the institution of confession there was no Judas present. In his resurrection and appearance to the disciples, the Lord drew all the members of his Church out of their state of alienation, from their cursing and denial of him, from their guilt and indifference, and set them back right into his own state of purity from sin. His very appearing had the effect of confession as much as of communion, and his word on that occasion imparted the Holy Ghost (confirmation) and, at the same time, the power of binding and loosing (Holy Orders). He himself is the Anointed, who had died, and who had been consigned to his death, so that, dead and now risen, he unites in himself all the sacraments as their source; only, there is here no express mention of matrimony, which still remained concealed in the mystery, subsisting from the beginning, between bridegroom and bride. The Lord concerned himself expressly with his chosen priests, who were to be his imitators both in their life and their office. This explicit attention of his to the hierarchical element and to the following of the cross is in line with his explicit institution of the sacraments.

The central sacraments are communion and confession. Communion is Christ himself, in the form in which he appeared after death transfigured, and which it embodies; but confession is situated in the very centre of his acts and utterances, and opens everything else to our view. Communion is what he is; confession is what he does.

The visible Church as an institution and in its hierarchical character acts, in a way, like a framework. The sacraments are situated in the Church and are communicated, as its living content, through the official channels. They too, as a consequence, have a certain rigidity about them; they are in danger of becoming institutionalized. The person receiving them is, indeed, aware that he has to do something positive, but that is very slight in comparison with what has already been done and what he finds there. This applies least of all to confession. Here it is not enough for him to go to church and listen to something or suffer something to be done to him. It is his confessing, contrition and purpose of amendment, in literal fact, not as a ceremony that are required. The reception of this sacrament, too, is far more a matter of his own judgment and reflection than that of the others. In consequence, a state of vacillation arises which is not experienced otherwise. One knows one will have to confess again some time, but when? There may be sound reasons for not going at once. We need to be inwardly alert and watchful to know when the proper time has come; and this requires a certain Christian maturity and responsibility.

The basic character the Lord imparted to his Church was one of enduring vitality and mobility. This character was not only given to the Church as a whole, but each individual member has a share in it. The Lord became man to manifest to us the intense life of the Trinity. This manifestation does not cease with the Ascension or give place to a period of institutional rigidity, but is continued in the vitality of the Church through all times. Nor is the element of vitality present for the sake of the organized framework, but the framework for the vitality, which reaches out through the whole Church into the personal life of all the members. This mobility is most clearly seen in relation to confession, in the personal participation in it, in the mutual interaction of Church and penitent. And as his living intercourse with the Father in the Spirit does not prevent the Son from being fully man, but, in fact, makes him perfectly so, the Christian in confessing is not thereby less a man, but rather more mature and responsible. The act in which he participates to receive absolution is, indeed, of divine ordinance and so pertains to the sphere of the institutional Church. It is, none the less, something personal, a matter of individual responsibility, and thus fully human.

Original Sin – Confession – The Church

Original sin is active within us, and causes in each of us a predisposition, an inclination, to actual sin. Often it happens that someone makes a resolution not to sin, and falls again, but only realizes it afterwards. It is as if in man there were two personalities, each dominating in turn. One of them gives the warning: don't do that, it is a sin! This one keeps the upper hand as long as the man pays attention to it and is determined to follow its advice. But then, suddenly, he turns away. Hardly has he prayed: "Lord, I will to do all that thou willst" than he sinks into a mood of indifference, does precisely what he ought not to, forgets the Lord, gives up praying, acts uncharitably to others. But when that time is over, the time when charity is impugned and God ignored, he realizes what he has done and repents. It is as if he were accompanied by some evil power, possessed by a will unconcerned for the things of God. In addition, there are a number of sins that he commits deliberately, but very often even here the real cause is a reluctance to reflect properly. Fundamentally, there is the will not to do the thing, yet it is done. The flesh is weak because the spirit is not vigilant enough; it can only be kept vigilant through constant prayer. A Christian may know from experience that he finds peace and refreshment in prayer and the thought of God; but in spite of that, he gives them up, not because they are burdensome, but through indifference. He lets opportunities for prayer slip by, on the ground that there will always be others. Often it is not a question of sin, simply of unconcernedness. He may behave as a good Christian, and value the means of grace offered by the Church. But what he values even more is his own tranquillity and immunity from anything disturbing, even when the disturbing factor is grace. It is only at moments of fear at having lapsed so far that he realizes his true state, his subservience to sin, a state, whatever form it may take, of want of charity and so of enmity to God.

Even if someone goes to confession again after such a short time that there is no question of his having forgotten God in the interval, and cannot find anything to say, yet he is bound to admit that, even so, there is some element of forgetfulness, some lack of perfect vigilance, some want of response to the urgent promptings of grace. Our knowledge that we never really correspond to grace might well induce despair, if the grace of confession, the Passion of the Lord, the resources of the Church in penance and prayer, were not of such immeasurable value and efficacy.

Confession means a great many different things, in addition to the enumeration of one's sins, exciting contrition for them and receiving absolution. It is meant to give, also, an insight into the needs of the Church, so that mankind's enormous deficit as regards grace may be, in some measure, reduced. This deficit is present even with the holiest; perhaps they feel it more than others. Once we perceive this enormous need of the Church, our own need becomes somehow depersonalized; it becomes a need to give something to the Church. What may well happen then is that my own ever-present deficiency, arising from original sin, is changed into one that results from my having parted with something in favour of the Church. The Church needs it, and its gain involves a loss to me. This, of course, does not mean that I can look on the results of original sin as something unalterable, a matter of indifference, and so go on to increase them. On the contrary, I have to try to reduce the area of indifference, so as to give the Church something to lay hold of there. And what the Church needs is that the following of the Lord should be achieved, not only in a kind of triumphant progress, but also in grief, trouble and weakness. Recognition of our powerlessness is only a small part of humility, which is not ultimately a matter of knowledge. It is much more something the Church gives to one who knows what he lacks, when she accepts his gift. He is too concerned with the Church to reflect on his own state, and it is the Church that, in a sense, infuses into him the virtue of humility.

So we see once again that confession always has a social, ecclesiological side, and that the individual himself has to make his confession as a part of the Church. The Church is a unity that builds itself up in her sacraments. It is never just the sum-total of Christians, never just their ordering and organization before God.

6. THE PENITENT

Exaggerated Views

Every child who has been prepared for his first confession knows that he is a sinner and has to confess, and that a single confession does not settle the whole matter. He knows too that, with his first confession, he is given a particular place in the Church, attains a certain maturity as a Christian, and takes on certain responsibilities the scope of which is not seen at the time, but becomes more and more manifest. The confessions made in early childhood are, perhaps, the best, because the child is conscious of its faults and, at the same time, has a sense of being initiated into something sublime and elevated. Later this sense is, to some degree, blunted with most people. Confessions, when they follow at fairly regular intervals, gradually lose their mysterious character, both as regards sin and as regards participation in the life of the Church. But the adult often still realizes that his childhood confessions were the most valuable, and that he must make use of his present knowledge and perhaps his greater immunity from self-delusion to recover a deeper sense of the mystery and of the magnitude of the gift. A good confession that puts one's life into proper perspective remains effective a long time afterwards, not so much as something remembered from the past but as an ever-present reality, a precious gift active and living, which one feels in duty bound to protect and preserve.

Certainly, there are many who regard confession as an unpleasant but necessary duty to be performed only at the prescribed time. The Church lays down the rule of Easter communion and is satisfied with confession once a year at the same time; and so the mediocre Christian thinks that he has no further duty beyond this. Whether he is aware of it or not, his practice is a kind of insurance. He is conscious of a number of sins, but looks on them, as a more or less normal part of life, and the annual purification equally. He makes no claim to be specially devout, but is quite prepared to perform the unpleasant act and accept the humiliation, provided it is not demanded of him too often. He goes to confession in a calm, calculating spirit, though it is not as if he were not sorry for his sins or that his confession were incomplete. But, if he has made it a rule not to confess more than once a year, his confession will scarcely have any noticeable after-effects. The one redeeming feature in this unpleasant act is that once done it is over and finished with, and thus any further efficacity is not at all desired. Confession is one of the things one does not talk about or even keep before one's mind. This is, perhaps, a masculine attitude: with no understanding of the personal side of absolution, its relationship to the Lord, of how his grace prompts to further efforts. If confession is nothing more than an unpleasant duty, it is something to get over and forget; to remain receptive and docile to its continuing action would be effeminate. Those who think like this are chary of all talk about religion. They speak about it as seldom as they would about a small sum of money they may have put safely away. Those are private matters. They look on the confessor as an official not so very different from a bank employee; they both discharge a definite function, paid for, in the case of the confessor, by the penitent. Both are part of the way society is ordered. And just as the balance-sheet is drawn up at the end of the year, so one settles one's account with God and his spiritual official annually and begins afresh. Any physical need is met by the bank-book, and spiritual needs are provided for by confession. We do not expect the bank to augment our credit balance suddenly; neither do we expect any similar spiritual increment from the Church. The whole thing proceeds on a familiar, determined pattern that admits of no elasticity.

Contrition, too, is conceived by such people in a similar commercial spirit; it is because confession costs them something that they feel distress at having committed this or that sin. It may well be difficult to decide whether they are more sorry that they will have to confess it on account of the offence to God. They do not examine themselves very closely on this, nor on matters of fraternal charity, nor on their care and concern for wife and children. Their examination of conscience is conducted in a detached sort of way, and, however uneasy their conscience, their contrition is kept well within certain bounds fixed beforehand. They do not set much store by the instruction the priest gives. Since it is not of the essence of the sacrament, it might as well not be there. They are ready to make a proper confession, but not to be probed too closely; nor to let themselves be overborne by what the confessor suggests, and led along awkward ways. It is quite possible that they have already experienced what happens when they take his advice to heart and apply it to their own life; but now what they want is to remain undisturbed and tranquil. So they make their confession in tranquillity, in the way they want to and as they have arranged beforehand. As for resolutions, if they are at all serious, they are primarily self-centred. The penitent may be afraid at finding, in the course of his confession, that he is further from God than he thought, that he has been guilty of more sins than he bargained for. So his resolutions take a rational form, as if he should say: "I must not go on like this; I shall have to watch my step a little." If he looks on confession as an insurance-policy, he is prepared to pay the premium, anxious not to fall into arrears or to do anything which might raise difficulties about the paying-out. In all matters of insurance there is a certain risk which is not covered. In this case, if he has chanced to have sinned too greatly, he would not be covered by last year's abolution. He must not let that happen. The idea gives him a sudden shock, and he sees that the state of the business looks rather different from what he had anticipated.

The opposite extreme is the scrupulous person, who never finishes with confessing the same sins. He also looks on confession as an insurance, but does not know its conditions exactly. He is harassed in mind because he does not perceive God's grace, and undervalues this grace inasmuch as he looks for reassurance on human grounds. He overestimates himself in thinking he is in a position to weigh up his own words correctly, and that God is not able to draw the right conclusion from his own imperfect, halting confession and to make straight what is crooked. He imagines God is not satisfied with the explanation given, that each explanation requires further commentary, and also that he, as penitent, is certainly incapable of understanding correctly what the confessor says. Misunderstandings lurk everywhere. He trusts God as little as he trusts himself. Contrary to the former type of penitent, he knows no finality. In reality he persists in his attitude of knowing better than the confessor, and precisely because of this attitude he asserts over and over again that the latter has understood nothing, and that God cannot have anything to do with such a confession as he has made. His chief sin, however, his want of trust, is very difficult to bring home to him. He is convinced of his guilt, but even here he knows best, and is quite unable to distinguish where his guilt really lies. So he goes about from one confessor to another and takes every opportunity to confess, but can never see absolution as setting him free to start a new and better life.

How should one deal with the scrupulous? If the confessor, after the first or second confession, is uncertain what is the cause of that state, he should be rather lenient for the time being, for the symptoms may, in some circumstances, be connected with an experience of conversion. But if he is certain that it is a case of pure scrupulosity, then the only thing is for him to be absolutely firm and unyielding, and at the same time to show great kindness. On the whole, a rather too frequent confession is better than going too seldom; the correct number might be fixed so as to seem somewhat excessive to the confessor and somewhat inadequate to the penitent; but, once decided, it should be strictly adhered to. Great emphasis should be laid on the exceeding power of God's grace. The actual confessing of sins should not be played down in such a way that the penitent gains the impression that his sins are not being taken seriously. Sin in all its forms must be taken seriously. Paradoxical though it may seem, the confessor may well hold that sin might have been committed in a greater number of instances than the penitent thought, in order to show him that the final decision is not his. It is, in fact, clearly the desire to have the last word that makes the penitent so often add to what he has confessed, revert to earlier confessions, demand shorter intervals between confessions. For that reason, it is better sometimes to exaggerate rather the number and gravity of the sins to make the penitent realize that it is sinful to be so much attached to one's own opinion and to minimize the rôle of the confessor. But once the confessor has judged the gravity of the sins, he should point out how grace abounds still more and thus reserve the last word to himself, since it is the Holy Ghost that speaks through his office. The ultimate emphasis must always be on the ever greater measure of grace.

We constantly make the mistake of looking on the scrupulous person as too weak; for he is also too hard in so far as he persists in his attitude of knowing better to the point of putting up a granite-like resistance. In some cases, one may suggest a short scriptural text that states plainly that grace is stronger than all else. One may also try to make him face the question why it is that he goes to confession, whether through love of God or love of self. If through love of God — which he certainly wants to be the case — then surely he must see that from it flows out the superabundant love God has for him. The confessor must be patient during the penitent's confession, but the advice he gives must be firm and definite.

The cure may be a sudden one, in which case it is purely the work of grace; but generally it is a gradual process. As a rule, scruples are a sign that many other things are amiss in a person's general attitude. They may be the expression of a real neurosis, of a tendency to self-absorption which can find no other means of satisfaction and here, at last, has discovered a way to make oneself interesting.

The Right Attitude to Confession

Every Christian is conscious of his sins and imperfections. He knows they are the result of his own special tendencies and weaknesses, his own want of care and recollection, and that they are of almost daily occurrence. He knows too that he is quite capable of greater sins, even though seldom guilty of them. If he has not been to confession for a long time, he feels that he has withdrawn himself from God. He can specify the points where he has, to a greater or lesser extent, gone wrong, and even when he has not committed any definite sins, he is conscious of a general negligence which shows plainly that he is always capable of and, in some sense, ready for, sin, and that it is perhaps only a special protection, a special grace, a lack of opportunity that has kept him from it. Others, his brethren, have been less privileged, and he feels a solidarity with them, indeed with all sinners. Were the circumstances of his life the same as those of any particular sinner, he would very probably have committed the same sins. Yet the sins of others do not serve to make him excuse his own, or to look on them all as a general social phenomenon. On the contrary, they intensify his sense of his own sinfulness, and show him, as in a mirror, what he would be capable of without the protection of grace. Something of this "communion of sinners" should be felt whenever one goes to confession, though there can never be any question of confessing sins one has never committed, or for which one has no direct responsibility.

Of course, in the case when someone falls suddenly into grave sin, he will not wait till his usual time before going to confession. But at all times he must remember that the sacrament does not work mechanically, that he is subject to a judgment, which may be either of binding or loosing. Nor should he forget that it is possible that his sin, for good reasons, may be retained. Otherwise, he is in danger of ignoring the element of humiliation that is part of confession, and of playing the part, to some extent, of judge over his own sin. In any case, he must always be ready to do more penance than is prescribed. What preserves him, also, from the danger of making himself the judge is prayer, which should be the setting of his whole preparation for confession; for he should examine himself and estimate the gravity of his sin, not in his own light, but in that of the Holy Ghost. In that light, the only true light, his contrition will be more profound and truly supernatural.

The absolute openness so necessary in confession does not preclude a certain discrimination. We have to confess according to the way the matter appears to us, and eschew undue elaboration as well as theorizing about oneself. It may happen that, in the course of confessing, one loses the thread, forgets details, the things come out in a different order or in none at all; or something incidental suddenly seems important, because, perhaps, one feels overwraught or else because the Holy Ghost wills a certain feature to be emphasized. None the less, one must know there is a duty of obedience to the actual ordering of confession, adhere to the matter in hand, and not try to force oneself to express things otherwise than they appear, nor insist unduly on any particular matter. Each sin must be called by its proper name, without exaggeration on one side or the other. The priest has to know what the matter really is, and should not be burdened with the products of fantasy.

Faith in the Power of Confession

The Lord's Ascension into heaven seemed to sever a connection that had existed till then; it ended his life on earth among us sinners, his involvement in this sinful world. This breach at the Ascension is an image of the effect of absolution; for we too, after being absolved, cease for a time to be what we were, a connection is broken, a world is left behind, our soul is, for the moment at least, free for its ascent to God. It knows itself no longer, since the breach with what it was previously is absolutely real; what seemed tangible before and pervaded by sinful meaning is seen to be illusory and has lost its efficacy. We are free, with a freedom that has its source in the Son at his Ascension; and this freedom orientates us to God, to a better life for the future, to newness of being. It may be that the after-effects of our sins remain with us, but it is not as if they kept the vital energy of the sins to which they belonged. And even if, by the divine sentence, we have still to atone for our sins, we must do so in the spirit of our new childhood. "The cord is broken, we are free." We cannot understand the main significance of confession apart from this breaking of the bond; but it is not chiefly a question of our understanding, but of our faith prompted by charity. This it is which has been changed, enabling us to see with fresh eyes, and giving us a new insight into what love is.

The Lord carried our sins to the Father, and his bearing of this burden as he hung on the cross constrained him to the point of death. Only in this way was he able to efface our sins. Once again, on Holy Saturday, their full and terrible burden was made manifest to him; and that was the condition for his experiencing the lightness of the Ascension, of a departure to the Father free of all burden. It is the same lightness, the same release that the Lord grants us in absolution.

How many Christians, including priests and religious, leave the confessional without any sense of joy and alleviation! They have acknowledged their small daily sins, their irritability, impatience, discontent, harsh speaking, all the pettinesses and meannesses that disfigure their ordinary actions; they have confessed them, because one must make one's confession. But they come out unchanged, because they have no desire to see or believe in their disengagement from the past, or, at the most, perceive it momentarily in the confessional, only to rejoin at once the sorry image of themselves that they have dragged about with them from time immemorial.

They do not really take in what the confessor says to them. It is almost as if he were addressing, not them, but an image of them, which is then immediately submerged. They have no inkling of the joy of the Ascension, the joy of being cleansed that Peter knew when he desired the Lord to wash, not only his feet, but his whole body. For many, on the contrary, confession is simply burdensome. In the case of the laity, it is often just one more burdensome element in their life as a whole, in the way they have chosen, with all its narrow, unalterable relationships. They do not see as clearly as priests and religious what being a Christian really is, the Christian image, what its potentialities could be, how it is darkened by their own sins, how it has to be protected, and in what directions it is capable of growth. This inability is the cause of their despondency, and they are not freed from it in confession.

This image is more easily descernible by those in religious communities, by reason of their rule, which, through the spirit it expresses and the way it indicates, ought to be a source of joy to them. The rule itself involves the separation from the sinful world merited by the Ascension; but it has to be lived, and that means conflict and, above all, the use of confession to that end. That is what so many forget, and why the rule seems to them dry and lifeless, if they think about it all, and if it is at all clear to them that, at each confession, the rule offers them anew its power to tear them free of their bonds. All they have to do is to reach out and grasp it to be carried up by it into heaven.

7. TYPES OF CONFESSION

On Conversion

THERE ARE two kinds of conversion-confession, the characteristic of which is that grace not only operates pre-eminently in the short period of confession, but transforms the entire life of the penitent. It makes clear to him all the imperfections of his past, and convinces him of the absolute necessity of changing his life from the very root always with reference to a personal mission.

The first kind is when someone, at the very time of confession, is struck with grace, a compelling grace, which suddenly puts everything in a new light. If the grace is genuine, it will make itself felt to the penitent as stripping him of all rights and taking him wholly into its service. There is a harsh and relentless quality about it that does not bend to circumstances, but insists uncompromisingly on a new life. Generally, the confessor himself is made aware of this grace as strongly as the penitent, and understands that he is required, for his part, to take it in full seriousness and to direct the penitent accordingly. In many cases a particular vocation is manifested; in fact, that is the rule. But there are also cases in which the change indicated has to be brought to light and given shape and form, and where the status of the individual in the Church remains as before. The first kind is not specially prepared beforehand; it happens all of a sudden, and no one can say how far the previous life furthered or hindered it. The grace may equally well strike a hardened sinner or one striving after perfection. Such was the grace that struck Saul on the road to Damascus.

The second kind is not so sudden in its working; it may be the outcome of prayer and desire, may have been expected. The penitent may have been preparing himself for a long time for such a confession, have attached special importance to it for some intrinsic reason, or, indeed, for some extrinsic one, related perhaps to the confessor noted for his special insights. Possibly the penitent has gone a long way to see him. In such cases, the penitent will express himself so carefully, enter into such detail as to make it clear that he hopes this confession will be decisive for his way of life, will be something of a conversion and transformation. He is dissatisfied with his mediocrity, and sees that his life ought to be quite different. He presents himself with such urgency as to enable the confessor to cut the cord which binds him and, through his agency, the grace of God comes to satisfy his desire for a fresh start.

The penitent experiences the grace of conversion as something personal, but yet pertaining to the Church, which has its official representative as witness, and through him takes over its application. The person who is the subject of grace is by it made better able to serve God and the Church, joined to them by a new bond. The experience is imparted to him personally, and there is no call for him to go about publicizing it and drawing attention to himself as a "changed man". The fruit, however, of this "private" experience belongs wholly to the Church; the individual himself is not thereby taken out of the communion of saints, but rather inserted into it fully. Certainly, "by their fruits you shall know them", but know, not the person, but the Church made visible in him. What others want to see is not the experience but its results. These, indeed, will always fall short of what was demanded, but still they are to be wholly ascribed to grace. The person so converted remains an "ordinary man" whom grace has touched, and who will lag behind its stringent demands all through his life. The further he falls behind, the less is he able to set the standard for himself. Of course, one must not discourage him, but yet he must see, from the outset, what grace demands of him, and perhaps, by seeing it continuously in the light of the conversion experienced, he will easily come to accept it and put it into effect.

General Confession

There are three possible reasons for making a general confession. The first is personal to the penitent, who desires to settle up his whole past life, make an exhaustive revision of all that previous confessions should have concluded, and enable the confessor to view his whole life and provide help accordingly. The second reason may be the wish of the confessor. He has a penitent whom he feels needs to be directed otherwise than before or directed further, whose life he knows only in part, and needs to see more clearly and in depth. The third reason is entrance into a religious Order. The new state of life demands a comprehensive settlement of the past; the new obligation of obedience demands a complete self-manifestation.

There is one thing to be careful about in a general confession, more so than in ordinary confession, which is to ascribe to the sins confessed the character they had for one's conscience at the time. Two dangers are possible here. One is that, if I have not striven in the time immediately preceeding to live according to the will of God, I may not, in my confession, see my sins as they really are, but as slighter and less ugly. Or else I countenance certain verdicts on my life that are too complimentary, that do not tally with my past. Whether consciously or not, I might also influence the confessor by minimizing it all. The other danger is the opposite one that, through diffidence brought about by some previous decision or resignation to my existing condition, I describe the past as so charged with evil that it is evident that no good can be expected of me. That might well be a ruse to quell my inner disquiet or to silence the voice of God within me.

Every confession, but especially a general confession, must be made in an objective fashion; otherwise, the temptation is too great of seeking to justify oneself in one way or other, of using it to gain a factitious tranquillity that has no real foundation. The penitent must not gain the impression that, with his general confession, he has settled everything once and for all. That might involve him in pharisaism, the feeling that he has come to terms with his destiny, that he can enumerate his sins and gain a comprehensive view of them all. Whenever one prepares for confession, he must occupy himself a certain length of time with his sins, and so experience a kind of solitude within the Church. At a general confession, this solitude may be unduly stressed through misuse of the time given to the examination of conscience. For if this is prolonged beyond measure and the penitent thus detaches himself from the common life of the Church, he tries to create a personal certainty, whereas this can, in fact, be gained only in the life of the Church. In any case, this time should be largely given to prayer, which will prevent the intrusion of pharisaic self-importance.

Once the general confession is made, in whatever form, the penitent must not entertain the idea that he could have expressed the matter differently, and will do so at the next opportunity. It must have a certain character of finality, both as regards the self-accusation and in its aspect of a special grace. The general confession was, in fact, a real grace, and the penitent received it as such. But if he were to revert time and again to his self-accusation, he would be placing an obstacle in the way of grace. To desire to confess again immediately after a definitive confession would be to misuse grace; for it would mean ascribing importance chiefly to the human act of confessing, and not to the grace of God.

Finally, there is the general confession made in the course of a retreat. In a retreat one of the first things to do is to see one's sins as they are, quite apart from one's own assessment of them, objectively and yet as fully one's own. The sinner must come to realize that Christ bore his sins on the cross, that their enormity was such as to cause his death, the death of God made man. The relationship of Christ to sin throws an entirely new light on his relationship to the sinner, and this in turn affects fundamentally his view of his own life. In their effects both forms of general confession, whether on conversion or in a retreat, create new factors bearing on one's entire life. The results may be less striking in the latter case, but, in some circumstances, more enduring.

After the cross, the Lord gave the Church, as his first gift, the sacrament of penance. Then, for the space of forty days, he instilled into the apostles the meaning of Scripture and of the entire ordering of salvation, to send them, finally, out into the world. A retreat is a re-enactment of what was done first by the risen Lord.

Ordinary Practice of Confession

Confession during a retreat has a place apart in the Christian life, since its nature is determined pre-eminently by the meditations made and discourses given in the course of the retreat. But even the ordinary confession is directed to a definite end, which is not so much to make a clean sweep and set things in order as to bring added support to the individual in his life within a definite sphere, one which demands a certain degree of consistent purity from sin, so that he may offer prayer and sacrifice therein according to the mind of the Church. Its aim, in fact, is not so much to free the penitent from the bond uniting him with unpardoned sinners as to make him more capable of living as one of them, sharing their lot. Anyone who frequents the sacrament of penance solely to be absolved on his own account and to feel himself cleansed from sin, would be already tainted with pharisaism in his repugnance at seeing himself infected with sin and imperfection or being taken for just another sinner. He is one of those who are always looking on their own way as something out of the ordinary, who draw a line setting them well apart from sinners. In the Christian idea of confession, the desire is always present of obtaining a more intimate participation in the sinners' lot, of making the grace of absolution accrue to those who either have no knowledge of confession or do not practise it, and, equally, through frequent, even daily, communion, to obtain as much grace as possible for others. Preoccupation with the individual self must be avoided so as not to impede the flow of grace.

A person who goes to daily Mass and communion, and perhaps also makes a daily meditation or spiritual reading, will certainly feel the need to keep himself free from sin in a more than ordinary fashion, in order to live up to this. But if he only does these for his own benefit, he will probably consider his state is good enough and that God may well be satisfied with him, as definitely belonging to the ranks of the pious and fervent. If, however, he sees the apostolic obligation attached to these practices, he will be quite certain that, as he is, he is inadequate to fulfil it; it demands a higher degree of purity, which it is simply his duty to achieve. A man who has only his own interest in view will consider his shortcomings, such as his want of due reverence and so on, in these practices compensated by the fact that he is observing them at all. But one who acts for the benefit of the Church and the rest of men gives these a claim on him. They have the right to expect some positive result, something not rendered nugatory by a perfunctory kind of approach.

It is not easy to avoid every possible shortcoming in the practice of confession; in fact, it really takes a saint to steer clear of a pharisaic consciousness of one's own purity on the one hand and an exaggerated idea of sinfulness on the other. Psychologically, it is almost inevitable that frequency of confession should bring about a certain blunting of the sense of sin, whereas confession, of its very nature, ought to have the opposite effect. It should deepen one's insight into sin, which, indeed, is required if the act of confessing is to keep its freshness and vitality from one confession to another. Each confession should be, not just a "penitential exercise", but a new and more deeply felt act of humility; if it is not that, the absolute sincerity required may easily be lacking. To avoid slipping into quite a wrong attitude, a proper preparation is necessary, in which one attains a real conviction of the seriousness of the situation. No one can really confess if he imagines that between himself and sin there is a great gulf fixed. He must be absolutely convinced that he forms part of the kingdom of sin.

Confession of the Priest

The priest occupies a special place in the Church, inasmuch as he both administers the sacraments and receives them; he is concerned with them both in their institutional aspect and as sources of life. It is he who moulds the parish into a unity, a unity which is a gift from above and yet grows from below. This determines the character of his confessions as a sinner, as a priest who is a sinner. Like anyone else, he stands as a sinner before the Church's authority, to which he owes confession of his sins and his responsibility for them. At the same time, he is a person entrusted with authority, and it is left to him to conduct himself befittingly. This indicates the whole setting of his life, for, unlike members of an Order, he has neither a rule nor the spirit of an Order to mould him and instil a sense of what is expected of him by the Order in the name of the Church. For the religious, his rule acts as an intermediary enabling him to see more exactly and in detail the discrepancy between ideal and practice; the rule is the almost perfectly adequate mirror which shows a man what to confess. For the secular priest the sphere in which he can move as he sees fit is wider, he can form his own judgment on many things, whether rightly or not; he can lend the force of authority to this judgment, and, if he is remiss in any way, can cover up his sins with his own highly personal views. His sin can imply either the disintegration or triumph of such views.

The priest is accustomed himself to hear confessions and to absolve; this duty he has in common with many who belong to a religious Order. But though all sins may be said to be offences against the one commandment of charity, the sins of the priest are, for the most part, unlike those of ordinary penitents; in so far as they are conditioned by his milieu, they are, in fact, quite different. The sins of his parishioners are, to a great extent, such as spring from neglect of what faith requires: missing Mass and the sacraments, neglect of prayer, human respect, neglect of opportunities for apostolic work, indulgence in unlawful pleasures. The priest, through his office and its obligations, his distinctive dress, is largely immune from these. The danger for him is to be so taken up with the duties of his office that he gradually comes to lose sight of God's special demands on him personally. He may lose the sense of what the holiness of a priest should be, and become wholly absorbed by his external functions.

Hearing confessions should be an immense source of grace to him, of profit for his own confessions. If he applies his mind seriously in hearing confessions, he gains a keener understanding of what sin really is; for he has to judge as well as hear, and answer the questions arising out of what is confessed. All he has to do is to keep his eyes open, and he will see, in his penitents, both what should be imitated and what avoided. His penitents, in fact, are God's gift to him. Even if the sins arising from their condition are different from his, they must both share the same Christian attitude. This does not mean he has to imitate their confessions, but that he should always be able to gain from them some elucidation as regards himself. Here the influence of the communion of saints on those who are its official representatives and spiritual directors is especially evident, much more so than in the administration of the other sacraments.

A priest may have a penitent who confesses very correctly, and yet feel that there is something wanting; somehow his confession is made only in view of himself, without reference to the communion of saints. In that case, the priest must bring it back within that setting; and, when he himself confesses, conduct himself correspondingly, making his preparation, acts of confession, contrition and amendment all with reference to the communion of saints.

The Son, who while on earth, always stood before the Father in the attitude of a penitent, steadily drew his companions, the future Church, more and more into sharing that attitude. He did so most evidently when, on the Mount of Olives, he asked the disciples to watch with him. We generally look only on their failure on that occasion, but the main thing to be noticed is that the Lord wanted to see them associated with his Passion. The redemption was about to be enacted and confession shortly to be instituted. The representatives of the Church were invited by the Son to pray with him and share his sufferings. They were asked to work with him in founding the sacrament of redemption and so be able to be consecrated as he was, and then, when the Passion started, to possess a deeper, more personal, and also more authoritative, experience of it. He did not demand of them now, before the sacrament had been instituted, that they should join with him in confessing the sins of the world; but he desired to associate them with him, desired himself the support of their vigilance and prayer. Thereby the authority of the Church and the Lord's Passion were joined in closest intimacy. In that moment the Lord was the priest with authority, and the disciples were to be the Church, the communion of saints. When a priest asks his congregation to pray for him, he does, unconsciously, something like what the Lord did before his Passion. The request for prayers before Mass and on other occasions *(commendo me)* is very often not taken literally by priests; but the request is constantly reiterated, in union with the Lord, who desired not to abandon, but rather to continue, his human sufferings among his disciples, which, for those who shared them, would have been an infinite enrichment of their Christian lives. And when a priest prepares himself for confession and performs his penance after it, he is in a like position. He ought to realize what it means to give life by means of his confession as well as to receive it, to stamp on his personal act of confessing something of the character of the collective act of the parish and the Church, and, at the same time, give this latter something of the grace of his individual act.

This is, above all, a question of prayer. The priest may well ask his people to pray for him, but hardly to pray for his confession. Even the Lord only made a general request: Watch and pray, and told them the hour had come. He had no thought of demanding that they should "fill up what was wanting to his Passion". There is a certain sphere on which silence should be kept, but as it is open before God, the priest about to confess should petition God and the heavenly Court to look on his confession in connection with the people entrusted to his care, so that he may represent them, and somehow take them with him in his confession, and they participate in it. If he reflects on the tender relationship of the Lord to his disciples on the Mount of Olives, much in his own relationship to his parish will become, in the setting of the communion of saints, more true and more informed with charity.

The confessions a priest hears are far more numerous than those he himself makes. In hearing confessions, he listens to all kinds of sins, some of them of the most grave nature, disqieting him profoundly, and perhaps the feeling stays with him for some time. He has, of course, the grace of his office which protects him in this matter, but he has to use this grace in the right way. On the one hand, he must not apply it so as to enable him to put right out of his mind the things he hears, to have nothing more to do with them and to be left in peace. Nor, on the other hand, should he linger unduly on them to his peril.

In order to strike the right course, the confessor must consider the Son and his relationship with the Father. The only-begotten Son became son of man, depersonalizing himself in the humanity common to all. At the same time, this individual man, who is there looking to the Father, was "personalized" in the only Son of God. He was made flesh, and the body he took he had to keep intact over against the world, but while offering it continually to the Father in his function of redeemer. He was for ever gathering into himself his own being, flesh and blood, in order to spend it unceasingly. The Father willed that the Son should be this individual in the flesh, which should remain intact over against the world, even though giving itself up utterly to the world. And in so giving it up, he had to make the experience of what it was to be flesh, yet neither being so immersed in it as to incur pollution, nor reckoning himself as superior to it and shut off from it. These two elements in the Son, his body given up in the Passion and the sacrament, and his unique sonship in the form of man, are what constitute his special character as priest. Consequently, there the priest must look for his model, the priest who confesses those in his charge, and yet must make his own confession, so embodying in a single unity before the Father these two elements, the direction of confession and the total surrender to it. He gathers up the confessions, but he also disperses them inasmuch as he joins with the others in confessing, and so participates in their confessions. In making his own sacrifice he completes that of his penitents. He may seem to be governing confession, but as a true priest he must make himself subject to it. Herein he washes the feet of the Lord's disciples.

The penitent comes in his personal capacity, and in the confessional encounters the office; the priest comes as representing the office, and must bring his personality to bear. He can do so as priest only if he is himself an integral person; this he must be if he is to let the personal blend with the official. At Cana the Lord provided the best wine. As far as the miracle was concerned, any sort of wine would have done, or the water to have tasted like wine. But in going beyond what was necessary, the Lord was expressing his own personal judgment; he knew what good wine was, and wanted to give it. That is how the priest should act in confession, making it produce what is of greatest worth, and so himself becoming, according to God's intention, more and more personal, and the office yielding more enduring fruit.

In this way, he guards against treating his penitents all alike, all on the official level; not insisting they should confess as he prescribes, but letting them do so in their own way, freely. In each of them he should uphold, encourage and strengthen what is personal, so that, for their part, they may spend themselves more fruitfully in love. There is no greater danger for the confessor than to act officially, whether in hearing confessions or making his own. The danger is always present of looking at a sin, formerly clearly seen as such, as, through the passage of time, simply a familiar, recurrent failing, and, finally, only a formula repeated at each confession without any feeling for the concrete relation between the fact and the word expressing it.

In short, the priest administers the sacrament as confessor, and has it administered to him as penitent, and there is a risk that the former may make him lose sight of the latter. He guards against this by bearing in mind the Son's attitude, who kept intact his personal quality before men in order to place it at the Father's disposition for the world. For the priest this preservation of the personal means to be a man, to be alive, not just a compound of functions and things heard; also to be, what he perforce is, an individual sinner in the sight of God, and not a kind of end-product of all the absolutions he has imparted.

Confession of Religious

The situation of the religious in regard to confession is characterized by two things, which are plainly to be seen in our Lord's encounter with the rich young man. One is that the Lord enjoins perfection, an ideal envisaged by each of the Orders. The second is that the young man turned away from it, failed in his relationship with the Lord. Every confession made by a religious has, as its background, the tension between the ideal displayed and the failure in reality. They all know what was demanded of them, and equally are aware, not only in the abstract, that the reality always falls short of the ideal, and, further, that, in the concrete, the first who, according to the gospel, approached the Lord with the desire of perfection declined to follow the way indicated. Every religious, on going to confession, must keep this refusal in mind. Again and again confession recalls to him the terms of the Lord's demands, and that he must admit he has not come up to them. This sober certainty places him, from the outset, in a state of humility, a humility proper to the Order, and one which encloses him, all his life, a special atmosphere within which he lives and, in particular, confesses.

The individual confession of sin should fit in with the kind of humility appropriate to the spirit of the Order, and, in this setting, be also personal. This gives rise to a new kind of tension, between his own sins and the sinfulness of the Order as a whole, which falls short of Christ's demands, just as the religious state as such bears, through all time, the burden of the young man's refusal; this, in fact, far from diminishing, increases the individual's burden of sin, for he shares in it. Thus, besides these two refusals, there is a third, that of the individual in his quality of a religious, his personal failure as regards the ideals of the Order, a failure reflected in his personal sins.

Every religious foundation embodies one aspect of the following of Christ, but even the highest idealism at the time of the foundation cannot exclude a re-enactment of the course followed by the rich young man. From the beginning, the Order is encumbered with the burden of those who have not heard the Lord's call, and of those who, though they have come and know his demands, do not follow him in practice. It is a disturbing thing that the Lord pointed the way to Christian perfection, and that the first person would have nothing to do with it, and that every founder of a mode of discipleship is already burdened with the tragic dénouement always implicit in the gospel. It is a situation that harks back to the origin of Christianity, that the Lord offers such untold possibilities, and that the gift is rejected. And another disturbing thing is that, when the Order is already in existence, it cannot finally jettison the ballast which dragged the rich young man down, since the demands it makes are such that every individual and generation reproduces in itself this man, and is always conscious that a considerable number of the called have not followed.

Here, then, one confesses in the awareness of bearing along those who do not confess at all, and that the line of demarcation between the two is not sharply drawn. For the one who does not confess is like the member of a religious order, never giving all that is demanded of him, never keeping the rule as intended; investing himself through his vows with a certain appearance which his actual life contradicts. And it cannot be clearly distinguished how far this is due to the shortcomings of the Order and how far to his own. The Order too has, in fact, made certain concessions. Its first fire has died down, and for this, ultimately, each member is partly responsible. In the final analysis, therefore, the life of the Order consists in an impossible, anomalous synthesis between the word of the Lord and the non-word, the refusal of the rich young man.

The life, then, of the religious is largely that of bearing a burden, and this shows what his penitential attitude should be, whether he belongs to a contemplative or an active Order. The contemplatives bear the burden of this situation in their mode of life, and the active religious seek to change it in some degree in showing forth the Lord's call in all its exigency.

The religious state is, by definition, a life that chooses penitence as its enduring attitude, that hears the call to follow Christ, though his demands become more and more stringent, and so involve increasing failure on the part of the individual. The young man desired to follow, and only then did it seem to him too hard; it was because he desired it that the Lord pointed out the way. With all their failures, the Lord never ceases to show the way to the religious who remain in a state of willingness. The religious state offers closer contact than any other between the man who would like, but cannot, and the Lord who wills to give him access to all. And even when his own refusal becomes more and more plain to see, still his own offering to the Lord, his questioning and response, become more clear and explicit. This is the consoling factor in the midst of all the sadness. Even the man who refuses shows the Lord, by the very fact that he continues in the Order, that he wills the continuance of this opportunity, neglected though ever renewed. He remains, despite all his refusals, in the situation of love, more and more involved in it, an imperfect love, but ever present before the word of the Lord's perfect love. It is this continual contact that gives him understanding of the actual personal love of the Lord.

The confession of a religious must bring out his failure in the face of this love, specifically his failure as a member of a particular Order, whose basic characteristics must come to the fore in his confession. Despite, however, his failures, he must never forget that his vocation is to console the Lord for the falling-away of the rich young man, and of others like him. He will always be conscious that the Lord, to keep him from finally abandoning his course, gives him, day by day, abundant graces, so that he may seek ever anew, may persevere, reiterate his offering, keep before his gaze the ideal presented by the Lord. As he confesses in the bitterness of his heart, he tries to console the Lord for the bitterness of the young man's departure.

The difficulty of the religious life consists in that one should not experience consolation by turning away from the situation as indicated, but should have the courage to face it clearly, in order to bear it along with the Lord. However hard the burden laid on me by the Lord, I bear it with him. The religious life is, ultimately, a life of sacrifice, and it is precisely here that the sacrifice comes in. The religious must go through the fire of confession, in which the full extent of his failure is brought out. At other times, he may receive consolations from the Lord, as in Holy Communion; but here there is no indulgence.

If the Lord carried his cross for the redemption of all, and yet calls on his own to carry it with him, it is obvious that they do so in a Christian view, a view, therefore, that cannot take in the failures of others without according to one's own sinfulness its exact and evident place. In the confession of religious an essential element is to be representative (of the rich young man, and of all who find the Lord's demands too hard), but it is only so because the penitent in question is conscious of the gravity of his own sins. The Christian mode of acting for others knows no distinction between mine and thine. It means taking up what is thine into what is mine, so that it cannot be any more distinguished, in its essential qualities, from what is mine. This is not inconsistent with the religious standing at the point from where the rich young man took his departure, with his, therefore, being able, in a sense, to distinguish himself from the latter, in order, once again, to recognize himself in the one who made the refusal.

For this reason, the religious who is a priest and hears confessions is particularly required to shoulder the burden of their confessions along with his penitents, to take their sacrifice into his own, to include them expressly in his own confession. It is not difficult to see why St. John Vianney felt so strongly drawn to the religious life.

Confession of Contemplatives

There are two needs for whose satisfaction one may enter the contemplative life. One is the need of the Lord that there should be contemplatives, men, that is, who contemplate him, and devote their lives to this, not in idleness, but in severe travail of the spirit, which seeks and desires nothing but him, and finds in contemplation the way of access to him, so that the Church as a whole is brought closer to him, and the sacrifice of all comprised in that of these individuals. The second need is the desire to endure in anonymity, which, in fact, is more a concomitant of the act of contemplation than a part of it, an atmosphere surrounding the life of self-sacrifice in a contemplative monastery; it sees in the individual's effacement in the community both the sacrifice and its fruit. The first need is more that of the Lord; the second, that of the sinful world. The joint satisfaction of both is brought about in the contemplative life. The contemplative tries to be what both the Lord and the world need, what the Lord needs to save the world, what the world needs to be saved by the Lord, though it may not know it.

Here again must confession re-establish the original order of things. Contemplation as a chosen way of life permits of an especial intimacy with the Lord, and this presupposes a degree of self-surrender that enables the Lord really to reveal himself. The confession of contemplatives will be concerned with many things that, in the case of the active Orders or Christians in the world hardly matter, if at all, for of them is demanded a degree of inner purity which is often difficult to sustain. Confession should infuse new life into the effort to persevere in this, a new access of the stillness of contemplation, a fresh zeal to those who have become wearied, a new spiritual organ for the understanding of what the Lord deigns to show.

In ordinary confessions outside the religious life, it is generally the case that the penitent seeks to bring order into himself so as to be once more presentable. He thinks of confession as it affects him. The member of a religious Order, however, especially of a contemplative one, thinks primarily of the Lord. He should confess for the sake of the man whom the Lord wills to be purified, and who happens to be him. This again is all part of his desire to take part, anonymously, in the bearing of the impersonal world-guilt. Thus his attitude in confession is a real test of his seriousness in contemplation. The incarnate Son abode with the Father and looked on him in order to communicate his vision to his brethren. So too does the contemplative look on the Son, not to give him the joy of being looked on, but to help the world to come to the Lord and through him to the Father. This contemplative vision is the source of his vision in confession, the vision which confesses to the Lord, which joins up with the vision of sin seen through the Lord bearing and suffering it. The penitential and the contemplative attitudes call up each other, and merge together.

Contemplation is a powerful force, not only in the speculative, but the practical, sphere, and the contemplative has special need of a skilled confessor. We can never attend too much to the high value God places on the sacrifice of contemplatives, nor overestimate the range of its influence when performed as it should be. The confessor must be conscious of its far-reaching effect, not only theoretically, but through inwardly co-operating with it, a participation conjoined with the requisite theological and practical knowledge. The knowledge possessed by the ordinary sinner revolves round his insight into his personal sins. That possessed by the contemplative and his confessor centres on the need of the Lord, and this can be known only through a living contemplation. His contemplation must be such that it can be the living principle of his confession, and his confession such as to inform and animate his contemplation.

Confession in the Active Orders

What distinguishes those in the active life is that, through the power and mission of the Lord, they give themselves to their brethren. For this duty there is one permanent criterion. The active religious must ask himself, in regard to the persons or the office entrusted to him: Am I really the man God wishes to see in this place? Up to a certain point he can tell from the effect he produces, or from the way people react, where he falls short, whether in prayer, recollection, spirit of sacrifice, zeal. The contemplative sees in the Lord where he fails him; the active religious sees in men where he fails them. His prayer is directed, not solely, but in part at least, to the enrichment of his inner life, so that he may give himself to others in a more fruitful fashion. Of course, outward results are not the measure of his inner state, but yet an honest confrontation of himself with his mission will show up his defects. He should not pay attention to the talk, the disfavour, the superficial admiration of people, nor to the way his preaching or writing is received, but rather to the defects he feels in himself in his personal commitment, defects which are reflected in an often unconscious disappointment felt by others. This is the mirror in which he should look in examining himself for confession. Is it really the case that "virtue goes out from him" when he preaches, hears confessions, instructs and encourages souls? He perceives his defects, not so much in himself, but in what lies outside himself, what has been achieved; and this means, not the visible "achievement", but the relation between what could be expected of him in his apostolate and what he has, in fact, performed. This the penitent can see without much difficulty, but he may not be able to bring it home clearly to the confessor. The latter, for his part, if he exerts himself sympathetically, will sense what is meant, and not be content to brush it aside with conventional words of comfort. His own sense of inadequacy should lead him to understand that of his penitent.

When, then, the religious confesses, there is always a sphere which cannot be properly expressed, but is clearly shown by a sense of discomfort, to which corresponds a similar sense in the confessor, and springs ultimately from something wanting in the Order as such, the point at which the young man of the gospel went away. In all the feasts the Order celebrates there is an empty seat, and, though the gap is obvious, the feast still takes place. The chairs may be moved up closer, but everyone knows that someone is absent. It is all very well to speak of "representation", but what it implies must be clearly understood, and we have to be aware from the outset that stringent demands must be met if the Lord's account is to be balanced in the end.

Confession of Married Persons

The confessions hitherto considered were of individual members of the communion of saints. In the case of religious, confession was seen to include indirectly the shortcomings of the Order in question. But with married people, the other partner is included in a much more direct fashion, in virtue of all that comes within the range of married life. Admittedly, there may be faults on one side only, where one selfishly refuses what is asked and the other yields himself, but the question must be asked whether the demand and sacrifice of the latter were not equally selfish; or, again, if there has been some misuse of marriage, how far there was express or latent agreement by the other partner. In such cases, the confession of one party indicates that of the other, and the confessor, in the counsel he gives to one, takes into consideration its effect on the other. So the confession of one involves the accusation of the other, and the first one to confess enables the priest to test the confession of the other when it happens later. If both confess properly, they will derive from the spirit of the sacrament an understanding of their mutual position. The partner whose accusation is implied in that of the other will not consider it a betrayal, but understand that the confession, proceeding from Christian charity, could not have been otherwise; he will accept this, even if they had not talked over the matter beforehand. Each of them knows that in the confession of the other there can arrive matters of joint concern, that the absolution of one foreshadows that of the other, and that, in bearing the burden of sin together, they participate, in a special manner, in Christ's bearing of the sins of men.

We are all perfectly aware that God knows and sees everything; but it is quite a different thing when someone closely bound to me makes known to God my sin in confessing his own. That involves a certain humiliation, in that I do not know if he is doing it and how he expresses it. But he may show it to God in a new aspect, from a special Christian standpoint. Thus, for both parties, confession in the married state brings home strongly the fact of their presence in God's sight, and how his gaze penetrates to their most intimate relationships. Every sacrament tends to bring out how God is always present in human life; and this is particularly true of the sacraments we do not receive ourselves, but participate in only in virtue of the community of sinners and saints. But in the confession of married persons this aspect is especially prominent, and helps greatly to an understanding of the *communio sanctorum* and how one person can represent all others. When someone else shows God our sins as common to us both, it is almost impossible to draw a sharp distinction between mine and thine. Then we understand that, if there is a community even in evil, much more must there be in the good, and this applies to the good which is absolution. The sacraments have effects which go far beyond the bounds they appear to have in an external view.

The confession of married persons reacts on the sacrament of marriage, making then see more deeply how closely they are bound together in Christ through this sacrament, both in good and in bad. One part of their mutual love they can understand, another lies hidden in the mysteries of God. Even their confession should point to the fact of their mutual love; it is not a kind of limitation of this love through setting up an inviolable sphere of privacy, for, in that one takes the other with him into his confession, God, through the Church, knits the bond closer, makes their relationship deeper and richer. And the confession of one, ordering anew this relationship to God, makes the other also conscious of a new obligation to God and, in God, to his partner.

8. THE PRACTICE OF CONFESSION

The Testament of the Lord

CONFESSION is one of the fruits of the cross, as is shown by its institution at Easter. It is the perfect fruit, which always remains joined to the tree of redemption; for if confession is the Lord's command, a following after him, so absolution is his fulness of power. Confession was his gift as redeemer to his Church, the steward of his redemption. He gave it her complete by laying down its essential features through the words of institution and through their exposition in his own life and in the prehistory of the institution. He left to his Church the understanding of every particular contained in his gift; he entrusted her with the development of the sacrament on its practical side.

In the things he established he often indicated merely the outlines, and for the rest looked to the presence of his Spirit that he was to send into his Church. She would give stable form to what he bequeathed her only in the process of becoming. But the Church never builds in arbitrary fashion: she does so only in obedience to the principle of growth she has received, always conscious that what is hers ever remains wholly his.

He gave us the sacrament as a fruit of his life, and therefore as something living, which has to become alive in us too. It is a fruit that remains connected with sin, and he knew that, with us, it would never be otherwise, that we would be constantly coming up against the fact of our sinfulness. What he did was to make a way leading from sin to him. Sin was no longer to be simply an obstacle cutting us off from the Father; for when we sinners recognize that he bore sins for us, the way of expiation opens up straightaway before our eyes. It is true that sin is not something present of necessity, and that the cross does not change it into something good; but, once we have faith, we, as sinners, will be brought ever anew to the realization that "God is with us".

Preparation

The Son himself only entered on his earthly life after preparing for it. In heaven he made the decision to come into the world so as to show himself to the Father from there, and, along with himself, all sinners as well, bound together with him in a bond as close as he could make it. He desired nothing so much as for the Father to see in him the sins of the world, or even not to see him any more on account of the immensity of sin. To prepare himself for this he needed all the measureless duration from his eternal resolve up to his Incarnation in time and then, on earth, all the time of his hidden life of contemplation to prepare himself for the cross. That he could come before the Father so denuded, so open to his gaze, was not the least fruit of his preparing for it by prayer.

Even more does the sinner need to prepare for confession. In the first place, as a sinner, his view of the truth is blurred or blocked by sin. Secondly, he is always being invited by the Son to rid himself of his sins by confession, and that is only possible if the Lord himself imparts something of his own view of sin. For the sinner, then, preparation means to consider, in the Lord, his state of alienation, to contemplate the distance between himself and the will and being of God. In addition, he will recall his condition when he last confessed and was absolved, and see how different it has become. The sins, the cause of this change, he must continue to hold in view till he sees them with perfect clarity, their concrete circumstances, and their whole previous and subsequent history. As we examine and look at ourselves in this way, we know that God himself regards us with a look of mercy — for his will is to forgive — but a look that demands absolute truthfulness. We have, then, to make the sight of our sins as keen as possible, to set them in the piercing light of truth. We must be remorseless with ourselves, not so that God will be "touched" thereby and made more ready to pardon, but to be better equipped to serve him in the future. Absolution should be looked on, not only as a superabundant gift of grace of which we are wholly unworthy, but as a gift bound up with acknowledgement of the gravity of our sin; only so can we receive it in the proper way. This gift brings with it a profound humility; it is a gift that is intended to bear fruit and to train us to serve God better.

It is not enough for us to see our sins in the glaring light of truth; we must acknowledge them explicitly as ours and be utterly convinced that they are inexcusable, that God has given us sufficient faith and charity to avoid them. The perversity of will our sins show must be acknowledged, and our intent to commit them, to persist in them. If we try to excuse them, we become ourselves a hindrance to grace, and stifle, in great part, its working.

To prepare properly for confession requires a clear insight into Scripture and its practical application, in so far as it treats of the life of Christ and his inward feelings. Any of the events of his earthly life will serve as a starting-point for us to see into our own perverse condition. In all of them it is manifest that the Son lived by his relationship to the Father, that he was always the Son of the Father, purely and simply. We picture him to ourselves at any age, in any of the circumstances of his life; always he lives in an atmosphere of perfect sinlessness. We go on to compare ourselves with him, and see at once that we are unable to move freely by reason of our sins. He abides with the Father; his whole life is one of love for the Father, prayer to the Father, service of the Father. In his light we see the state of our life, our prayer and our service, what is wrong with them, what is missing. Wherever we look, we see signs of death rather than life, of lukewarmness, indifference. In all three aspects of our relationship to God, in love, prayer and service, our shortcomings will be manifest.

All this applies to the relationship of the incarnate Son to his fellow-men. He has left us "his commandment" of fraternal charity, not as an arid formula, but as the epitome of his whole life on earth. He loves us as himself, and, in this love, looks after us, reveals himself to us, shares in our life both of body and soul, makes us share in his, takes over our guilt, dies for us. He gives all that he has and can possibly give, but, in his love for us, he wills also to receive. We can compare with this our attitude to our own fellow-men, and discover how paltry our love is, how self-seeking and covetous, how much we have despised our neighbour, harmed, even hated him. The treasure God has entrusted to us to pass on to others we have allowed to decay. We have no choice but to acknowledge that all our sins against fraternal charity have estranged us from the Son.

Finally, we can look at the life of the Son in itself, his conduct in his own regard. It is always governed by his relationship to the Father and to us, and he never makes himself his own end. Whatever he allows himself, rest, recuperation, sharing in a feast, all that follows from his human nature is part of his free giving of himself. He rests to fit himself to work again. He rejoices, so as to be able to communicate his joy. In this light we see how we have exceeded or fallen short, and how this has hampered our vocation.

Though we must examine ourselves as truthfully as possible, yet it must be in no spirit of fear; it is, in fact, a grace that God demands this of us. As soon as we enter on the process of confession, even when we first start our preparation, we are under the influence of grace, in contact with grace. This itself should rid us of excessive apprehension. The examination should continue till the pattern of our sins is clearly seen, but stop when it promises no further fruit, when we begin to lose ourselves in a maze of considerations, when we find ourselves looking into, not just sins and their direct circumstances, but, so to speak, the circumstances of these circumstances; otherwise, we are in danger of falling into a new kind of sin, that of overestimating our own importance, of preening ourselves on our cleverness, and perhaps focusing our gaze on our "meritoriousness" in avoiding sin, instead of on the grace received.

There is, of course, the other extreme, of making the examination too superficial. The contemplation of Christ guards us against this too. The reason why our examination is too perfunctory is, generally, that we do not direct it according to what Christ has laid down, but according to our own ideas. These for some considerable time have been made to accord with our sinful state, to the lax principles of our environment ("everyone does it"), to a formalized pattern of confession rather than to the gospel teaching, or to a routine formula we use in all our confessions, the adequacy of which we never think of questioning. Instead, what we must do is to look at Christ, surrender to his truth, take him, his teaching and his life as the mirror in which to examine ourselves. That brings us to the essential truth.

Should we have committed a sin that we are not in the habit of committing, we must make a special effort to see it with perfect clarity. It is not so much a matter of examining its psychological causes at first (that will come later), but of seeing oneself infected by the sin; recalling, too, the certainty we used to have, frivolous or even culpable perhaps, of our immunity from it, and feeling the terrible humiliation of having committed it, none the less. If, on the other hand, we have fallen into sins we have the habit of committing, we must, first, attend to the circumstances and causes, the point where we went astray, the temptations and occasions to be avoided, and so to our relationship to God.

In preparing for confession, it is important to be strict with oneself in two ways: to acknowledge what really is sinful, and not to spend one's time on what is not. We must not, to humble ourselves more before God, magnify trifles which are not sins, things for which our conscience ordinarily does not reproach us. This would prevent us seeing our sins as they really are and make us incapable of bearing those of others. To assume imaginary sins in order to humiliate oneself more according to one's own ideas leads to a certain pride and upsets the capacity for bearing the burden of guilt. Deceived by false values we lose our perception for real ones.

It is important to remember that Christ himself devoted long periods to the contemplation of the Father, but none at all to the contemplation of himself. Contemplation, in fact, has always

God for its object, never oneself. If our examination of conscience has a wrong orientation, we take from God the time that ought to be devoted to him, and appropriate it to ourselves. It is useful to see that sins hinder our way to God, but the conclusion from that is simply that we should return to the right road as quickly as possible. Certainly, the confession of sins will, at times, turn out to be more summary than the examination of conscience; but even there the essential thing is to look on God, on the grace of Christ, which alone can reveal to us the extent of our ingratitude.

Take the case of someone really holy who quite certainly has done nothing wrong since his last confession. In spite of this, he would receive the grace of the sacrament in the same degree as anyone else, though he should confess only a single idle word. This shows that the grace of confession does not depend on the amount confessed. This grace, in fact, has a eucharistic character, it spreads out beyond the individual, and we should not, through an "exhaustive" confession, try, as it were, to exhaust the grace for ourselves. On the contrary, it is, in a way, part of the punishment of sin that the sinner must, necessarily, appropriate a part of this grace for his sins to be expiated, instead of letting it all flow out over the world.

The preparation for confession must be carried out, from beginning to end, under the guidance of the Holy Spirit. We must start by invoking him, asking him to act within us and show us the way, to be our true light, while we humble ourselves to become as receptive as possible. We ask him to be the judge and make us share in his way of seeing things. The same Spirit who will later effect my absolution is now to enlighten me, making contact with my spirit. All this takes place, not independently of me, but with my co-operation through prayer and the exercise of my own faith and reason.

Sometimes, one senses that a particular confession is made without any proper preparation. One or two things are just mentioned in a summary manner, which shows that the confession is not actuated by love. The whole attitude of the Father and Son to each other in the Spirit is an expression of love, and can only be imitated in love. Everything that the Incarnate Son shows the Father, even the apparently insignificant, he shows in the fulness of love, into which everything is integrated and from which it derives its worth. A person who confesses in a purely formal manner has no part in this love of the Son's. He confesses sins as if they were something abstract, self-contained, with no practical connection with him. That is pharisaism. It is almost preferable to hear the sinner hesitating over the gravity of his sin ("I am not quite certain . . ."), than a precise, assured statement. It is humility that matters most, and that is lacking in these cases.

In preparing for confession, there is, generally, no need of a special effort to discover one's sins. We know the points on which conscience is uneasy. They make themselves felt from the state in which we find ourselves, from the unrest, even the horror, felt at the time they were committed, from the anxiety preceding or following them, from the temptations we are subject to; all these are so many pointers to their presence and quality. Yet there is often a danger for us, in this procedure, of seeing our sins too much as embedded in our life and conditioned by our particular state, and of overlooking their objective character. The result, then, is that we fail to attain a real Christian sorrow for sin; we are sorry at our own misdeeds rather than that we have offended God. We have to learn to see them precisely in their sinfulness, and that will show us plainly the necessary connection, on the one hand of sinners with one another, on the other of all sins together. The importance of the sins committed is thereby enormously heightened, since one's own can no longer be seen in isolation, but only as part of a whole in which each sinner has become involved. The individual circumstances, mostly mitigating, lose their importance; sin is a single lump, indivisible. The absolute character of sin becomes evident; it is that to which God opposes an absolute negative, and I, the sinner, stand there within it. I have made sin so much my own that I now dwell right in its domain. In consequence, I cannot be separated from it merely by an act of the will; what is needed is God's grace of forgiveness, his absolution. However much the sinner may be contrite and confess, however clearly he views his sins, he needs, to be rid of them, absolution. In the preparation, the terrible thing is the discovery of how closely sinner and sin are welded together. The sinner longs to discard it, longs for purification, but before the words of absolution have been uttered, he cannot have the assurance that he will become other than the sinner he was. Nor can he foresee what sort of a person he will be when once he has been absolved. The sinner who goes to confession is home-sick for God; he is in exile and alone. Though a sinner along with all the others, he has no feeling of community with them. Only through absolution does he recover this sense of community, of the communion of saints, of dwelling with God. This new sense stirs up in him an understanding of those who are still exiled, estranged, seeking, isolated. Before confession he was so bound to sin that he could not understand himself otherwise than in that connection. After confession he is set free through being intimately bound to another personal being, that of God and, in him, that of each member of the communion of saints. This inmost transformation of the person is something he cannot achieve of himself; it needs the power and action of God.

Contrition

The Spirit which directs the examination of conscience gathers first the facts, and causes them to be seen as they are. The greatest possible objectivity must be aimed at. The sins must not only be felt weighing on us in their totality, but must be probed and acknowledged individually in their number, gravity and circumstances.

Only when this is done is it time for contrition, not before. The whole preparation for confession has clearly marked phases. If these are too much intermingled — as when one grieves for each sin straightaway on discovering it, and feels it so unbearable that one craves for absolution — then there is no possibility of seeing aright all the other sins. The clearsightedness that is the first requisite is derived from that of the Lord himself in all his attitudes and actions as regards the Father. He had come in order to suffer; but, as long as his hour had not yet come, he did not anticipate it, nor allow any foretaste of his passion to interfere in his present mission. From him, then, we have to learn to apportion our time. That does not mean becoming so absorbed and fascinated by the consideration of our sins that there is no room left for the act of contrition that should follow. The whole course from insight into sins up to contrition and resolution, from confessing to absolution, is quite clear and logical; and we must always know at what stage we happen to be.

Contrition means that we are horrified at the extent to which we are alienated from God through our own sins. In contrition there is no place for excuses and well-intentioned returns on circumstances and motives; no place either, at first, for good resolutions. We must confront our guilt as guilt and keep it resolutely in view. We must measure its extent, and that not only by seeing what we have done, but also by comparing it with what the Son always did on earth in relation to the Father, the uninterrupted attitude of love he had, which all the sins of men were powerless to disturb or to change. He bore sinners to the presence of the Father in so purifying a love that the Father saw in them all only the love and atoning spirit of the Son. There was nothing in the life of the Son, no burden, no fatigue, no journeying, no preaching, no miracle, that could alter his attitude of love. He made use of everything to draw him nearer the Father, so that, both the labour of his mission and the fruit of that labour became, through his vision of the Father, something of positive value in his sight. As we contemplate the Son's actions, his life day by day, he seems, to our human eyes, to grow ever nearer to the Father; and this nearness of his should make us all the more sensitive to our estrangement. Only by comparison with him can we measure our distance from God and how near we were when in the state of grace. When we thus measure our nearness and remoteness from God by the enduring nearness of the Son, our contrition will be, from the outset, related to God, a real Christian sorrow, seeking God. That we are not better than we are will not be a source of suffering and nothing else; for it is not by dwelling on our failures, but by looking on the Son, that we come to recognize our lack of love.

This contrition should be something painful; for, if it is Christian, it cannot just reside in the intellect. We are, here and now, the lost sheep. The pain must be in our heart, precisely where we ought to have loved and have not. No one can pray or meditate if he has just done an injury to someone. His meditation is bound to be quite fruitless; the Spirit will not show him anything, but send him out to be reconciled with his brother. We cannot pray or contemplate with the understanding alone; the whole man is involved. Likewise, the whole man must be contrite. Admittedly, one who is in a state of sin will find it difficult to gain any conception of the sinlessness of Christ; he will have lost all discernment for it. Yet by the very fact that he wants to confess he has the beginning of a return to God, of a recovery of his perception of God. He has at the very least a glimmer of hope that he can change his condition, even if he knows himself to be not yet converted, delivered. He is not absolutely in despair or resigned to his fate. When a person intends to confess, he is already touched by grace, though imperceptibly. Perhaps he does not take account of his own inability to reconcile himself with God, to find any kind of access to him, by his own power. Yet, however low he has fallen, he knows that God's power is greater than his weakness, that God can find a way unkown to him. So long as confession remains a possibility, God has not definitely broken with the sinner. Even though a man, not having yet confessed, cannot be assured of the entire love of God, there is still a remnant of faith by which he holds to this love, which cannot desert him and which makes contrition possible. He can, in fact, only be contrite in the setting of this love, though, for the time being, he has no access to it. This love, unfelt but ever present in faith, gives his contrition a distinctive quality. In its light he sees sin for the first time as sin, not just as guilt in a human, mundane sense. Had he sinned "behind" the back of God, it would all be far less bad; but he sinned "before" him, in the sight of his ever-abiding love.

This factor it is which must be represented as vividly as possible in the process of stirring up contrition. Before his very face I have set myself against him. The situation must be seen in all its starkness. There must be no attempt to ascend to some sort of abstract, ethereal region in this matter of contrition. We have to represent to ourselves simply how nakedly we stand before God, as the Son stood before the Father utterly devoid of concealment. Adam hid himself but was none the less unconcealed before God. Then we have to see what it means to have offended God to his face, God in the man Jesus Christ, who confronted sin, who, as a man, also confronts me when I sin; see, too, that, man as he is, he is at the same time God, and that his whole life on earth was conditioned by his life in heaven. In my contrition, I must encounter, not only the man Jesus, but the eternal God, by means of Christ's humanity. God gives grace and this I cannot possibly doubt; my very will to contrition is an effect of grace. As soon as grace takes hold of me in whatever way, it begins to spread out and leaven everything. I am the lost sheep, but, as soon as I see that, I know that I am not wholly lost; gone astray, indeed, but sought after. A child in the street may let go his mother's hand and remain concealed till she comes back. If she fails to see him and passes by, he is seized with fear that she cannot possibly turn round and look again, yet, at the same moment, knows the contrary, and, knowing this and fearing too, runs after her. This is the state of mind of the sinner seeking God, one of fear that God should abandon him but also assurance that he will never do so.

Thus the sinner is well on the way to perfect contrition, for his gaze is directed towards God. He beholds the absolute greatness of God, his love above all, and is overcome at the discrepancy of his own conduct, not so much on account of its consequences to him as on God's account. And it is God's looking on him, which is grace, that permits him to measure the extent of his estrangement, and so to obtain the real insight into God's being from which follows contrition.

Fear of God's punishment can, indeed, play its part; but it is not the presence or absence of fear that determines whether contrition is perfect or imperfect. Joan of Arc made her abjuration in extreme fear of being deprived of the Church's ministrations. Many a saint, too, was actuated by fear without being any the less perfect. The view of God's attributes may fortify a man, but may also, if it is God's will, overwhelm him, making him and all that is his seem annihilated before God's greatness; and this very experience of his may be the beginning of real insight into what God is. Contrition is imperfect as long as it is bound up with oneself rather than motivated by God. A child who steals an apple and falls from the tree may be sorry that he has broken his leg. He may also reflect that he could have killed himself, and who knows what God might have done to him? The first motive is purely natural; the second has something supernatural in it, but the step from one to the other is a slight one. He may fear the police in this world, purgatory in the next. The actual change only comes about when God is the motive. The kind of supernaturality which sees God only in relation to oneself is still a form of egoism. The essential thing is that one is on the way to the desire to see things from God's standpoint. Even if the sinner has only advanced this far towards contrition, he will, in confession, through the grace of the sacrament, the pure gift of the Lord, attain to perfect love and so to perfect contrition; the love of God for him will prevail.

If two people are united in love for each other, they naturally expect from that relationship a certain enrichment or fufilment of their personalities, and this enrichment implies growth, an increment. The relationship will not remain the same from one day to the next, but become intensified; it will change, not just quantitatively, but in kind. Supposing, then, they become estranged and are reconciled once more; they will expect, from their reunion, a relationship not precisely the same as before. If one of them was to blame for the estrangement, he will have to make more than adequate amends, not only admit he was in the wrong, not only apologize and make it clear that he recognizes his fault, but also give clear signs of repentance. He knows he does not deserve to be received back into friendship, and will try to conduct himself as regards the other even better than before the breach. For he is well aware that this did not arise only at the moment when he acted as he ought not to have, but that he had long been remiss and indifferent and taken the friendship for granted. When, then, the other sees new signs of generous love, when he is convinced his friend is sorry for what he has done and is thankful at being received again, the relationship will not begin again where it left off, but will be enhanced, made more intimate.

There is, however, the possibility that the one in the wrong is not very much upset by it, only admitting it to himself, or else apologizing in a perfunctory way that allows him to continue as before. In that case, of course, there will be no generous outpouring of love and forgiveness on the part of the other, at least not in manifest form, however much the offending person assumes it will be given. At all events, it cannot be fully effective, and the relationship cannot restart at the former level, but only below it.

But perhaps he makes no acknowledgement of his fault and simply waits to see what will happen. His conscience is, more or less, uneasy but he does not avoid his friend, thinking that the matter will settle itself with time. Why, after all, should he not be indulged in just for once? When the other sees him again, he will realize at once that his friend has not taken the matter very seriously.

These two latter attitudes, in contrast with the first, show how cavalierly the sinner can treat God. He feels under no obligation to show God he is really sorry nor, indeed, to admit to himself even slight regret. Consequently, any relationship of intimate love between himself and God must, sooner or later, cease completely.

On the other hand, real, heartfelt contrition may create in the soul such fervour that, by comparison, its previous state seems utterly lifeless. Everything pales into insignificance before the tremendous formative power of grace which God puts forth on the soul, as if for the first time. It is as if someone who had enjoyed all sorts of visions of the things of heaven, and then, at the end of his life, sees heaven revealed in such a heightened degree that his former experiences seem to have been only dreaming. Or perhaps he sees his mission in its consummation in heaven, and what he sees has no relation at all to his earthly mission; consequently, he cleaves to it no longer, not through virtuous indifference, but because he is so absorbed by the new one that the other falls away of itself. The new truth disclosed to him far excels the old. In the same way, when contrition really takes hold of someone, he looks back, not only on certain definite sins which he repudiates, but on his whole life as alien from God. He will have nothing more to do with it, since, so far from preventing these sins, it positively caused them. His new encounter with God makes him see his life in this light, and his whole past must be blotted out to give place to what he now sees is demanded of him.

Confession is closely related, by Christ's ordinance, to the new life he began after death; and so the penitent sees himself as one who has died and been buried, consummated, to whom the Lord has granted the power to be wholly detached from this world, just as he was no longer of this world between his resurrection and ascension. The Lord makes us here sharers in his eternal life, and contrition is a sign of the new eternal life that follows death to the old; it brings an element of eternity into our life in time. We receive not merely fresh graces, but, through contrition, are enabled to enter the sphere of eternity, attain a new assurance of eternal life through the operation of the sacrament.

If, after confession, we envisage the future as much the same as the past, our contrition is not as it should be; our faith is shown to be limited, because we look at ourselves and our weakness rather than God and his power. Confession, even the monthly or weekly confession, always brings a fresh accession of grace. If we draw little or no benefit from it, that is our fault, because we persist in our indifference and even go so far as to tax God with the lukewarmness and monotony of our life.

Purpose of Amendment

This should have its sources in the Son's decision to save the world for the Father, to become man in order that the Father might have someone on earth united with him in friendship. It should be based on the Son's strict adherence to this union with the Father all through his life, his doing the Father's will without the least deviation from it. As sinners, we have to form the resolution to make ourselves better, so that the Father and Son may find their joy in us. We know that it is the Spirit who restores us to the Son and the Father, the Spirit who wills to join with us in framing this resolution, who shows us, too, where we fail to come up to this friendship, and how it may be reborn in us. We know that God offers us this friendship, and that he only awaits our acceptance; it rests with us whether we resist his overtures or accede to them. For that reason, we must consider, in the Father's presence, how we are going to live henceforth. The circumstances, about which we have already said we should not linger unduly, come again into question, for they can serve as pointers to our future way of living. They should be reflected on for as long as is useful for forming good resolutions, considered as concretely and as personally as possible; in this way we can derive from them concrete possibilities of improvement. Of course, it is not a question now of embarking on a fresh examination of conscience; we are at a stage beyond that. Still, the resolutions ought to proceed from the contrition, just as, later, they will find in confession their validation and confirmation. The resolutions are the element in the sacrament which should influence most our future way of life; they have to be carried out in practice. Whether, and how far, we have done so is the measure of our progress from one confession to another. Consequently, when making the resolutions, it is permissible to glance at our progress.

It would, of course, be pharisaical, when confessing our sins, to allude to the progress made: "This week I only lied three times, but five the week before." It could well be that, in God's sight, these three are more serious than the five. The important thing is that there should be a real purpose of amendment; if the contrition is genuine, the will to carry out the resolutions in earnest cannot be lacking. We should never be content with vague generalities: Things cannot go on like this! There must be some improvement. The question remains, what must be corrected and how?

My contemplation of the Lord's perfection necessarily reminds me of what I myself am, and the conclusion follows, equally necessarily, that I must not continue the same. That is only a survey of the situation in general terms, in the first place. Then, when my sins are recognized and repented of, and I experience deep humiliation at what I have discovered, another thing follows of necessity, namely that the resolutions must take concrete form. Contrition has, as it were, ploughed up an abandoned, overgrown field, and made it ready for replanting. Of its very nature, contrition demands a resolution to amend; that is its natural outcome. The resolution proceeding from it is not intended to bring tranquillity; it is rather directed to a definite action required by contrition, one as real as the sins are which are shortly to be confessed, and which are far from being imaginary. I myself have committed them, in a particular situation; and, since I remain the same person and the situation will, in some way, return, I must take definite measures not to fall again into the same sins. The moment comes when everything must be made concrete, if the purpose of amendment is genuine; as concrete as the Son's resolve to die on the cross.

Once again, two worlds meet in the purpose of amendment, just as, in the Lord's purpose to become man, heaven and earth, two worlds separated by sin, were perforce rejoined. Now it is I who must bring my own world, a world of sin, into harmony with the Lord's world, with the eternal resolve of the Son. From the eternal decree of God to its execution there leads a plan, a decision, that enters into all the details; it must proceed in this way and not otherwise. The Son kept to this plan. He viewed the different situations to which he would be exposed, not only experiencing them as man, but knowing them beforehand as God. The sinner, too, knows in part the situations in which he will find himself again, not so much their external, as their internal, aspect; he knows himself and how he is accustomed to react. He knows his weakness, but also that improvment is a quite real possibility. His improvement, his choice of the right course, is a real possibility foreseen in the Lord's plan of salvation, as real as the advance-plan of the Son's own life. In faith this possibility of ours in Christ has to be made as real as Christ himself, the content of our faith; and Christ knew, in all the resolutions he made, that it was always the Father's will he would do. We, though sinners, are able to insert ourselves into his acts, for that is our true place.

We must give concrete form to the different circumstances

and hold firmly to the resolutions made accordingly. If our contrition is real, it must have this result. In addition, we should adopt definite stages along which to advance, fixed points on which to take hold. It is all very well to strive for perfection, and the Lord certainly wills us to be perfect; but, if we only had this ideal in view, we would, when the first flush of enthusiasm was spent, soon sink into lassitude, and even despair. We must keep to particulars: how am I to avoid this or that in the future, despite the dangers and my tendencies? Making the thing concrete means to choose certain points to aim at. They should not be too many, if we are to achieve results. In addition, there must always be a clear awareness that keeping resolutions is the effect of grace, which we must, therefore, pray for. Consequently one of the resolutions must always be to pray better, and with that we can begin at once.

The consciousness that eternal life is present here and now is what animates us to carry out our resolutions, since they are themselves to be put into effect here and now. Even things that will only be put into effect the next day or week are to be performed at once in so far as the attitude corresponding must be practised now. Here, too, we must turn our eyes to the Lord, and see how, in his life, he gave reality to everything beforehand, with such assurance that he could anticipate the fruits of what he had decided upon: "Drink this blood which is shed for you."

The words spoken by the Son on the cross, "I thirst" and "My God, why hast thou forsaken me?", do not merely express his suffering at the time, but also reflect the attitude every real penitent should have. The sinner who receives the sacrament which is the fruit of the cross, who stands before the Father naked and uncovered, must have a thirst for absolution and for the nearness to God forfeited by sin. If he confesses in openness and humility, this thirst and longing will be granted him by God as a gift of grace; it will not be something he has worked up alone and, as it were, produced from within himself. This grace is, perhaps, less active at the time when he begins his examination of conscience, while his attention is wholly focused on himself, than when he begins to take cognizance of the outcome of this examination, of how he really stands in relation to God. His will to purify himself changes then into a longing to be purified, and this only God can satisfy. Only when he has received absolution does he see sin in its objective magnitude, as something that no longer adheres to him personally, but from which he still has to dissociate himself in a deliberate act. This repudiation of sin is not quite the same thing as contrition and resolution. Sin, even when confessed and absolved, will always remain, to some extent, present in his memory, as something of which he was capable once. Yet he must not dwell on it continuously as indicative of his own capabilities and what he is likely to do, but see it, rather, as a reality in itself, from which he is now freed, and which God himself has removed to the place assigned to it by his will. The ardent desire of the sinner for absolution should bring about an enduring result: a continuous seeking after God, which is, on earth, the true indication of love and a following of the Son in his suffering and "confession" on the cross; he, indeed, never ceased to thirst, till all was "consummated".

The sacrament of penance is not a psychological procedure, designed for the purpose of self-scrutiny and self-knowledge. It is concerned with bringing man close to God, and that is achieved through his effective will to show himself to God as he really is. The state of the penitent throughout approximates, through the grace of the Trinity, to that of the Son on the cross.

How to Confess

In going to confession, one should ask oneself the question: what is it that I am about to do? We should remind ourselves that the sacrament was given by the Lord and what it had cost him. It is his gift to each individual sinner, but primarily to the Church as a whole. For that reason, we confess as members of the Church, the community, and we have to take the community along with us and include it in the action.

First, we go to a confessional, where they may be many others waiting. In preparing ourselves, we should feel we have a share in all these confessions and commend them to God, also that ours is shared in by the rest. At the moment, we may feel tense and apprehensive at the prospect of this humiliating act of confession. In spite of this, we should take whatever comes our way in the course of waiting, whatever goes against the grain, in a spirit that deepens our understanding of the community of the Church in confession.

At last our turn comes, and we enter the strange atmosphere of the confessional. This place in semi-darkness is a place of grace; we are alone in it and yet part of a community; we are there and the Church is there. When someone goes into a church, he lowers his voice by a spontaneous impulse; he is caught up by the presence there; still more so in the confessional, which is the place of the Holy Ghost. It is also a place of fear, since there is a real danger, just before confessing, of a feeling of false pride creeping in that would like to stop us humiliating and accusing ourselves. Children are often attracted by the idea of confession, but adults find it repugnant. It gives children a feeling of being grown up, since they are now allowed to go to confession, a natural, spontaneous reaction. There is nothing spontaneous in the case of adults; they are inured to the procedure, and aim at getting it over as quickly as possible, pressing forward as if in a shop to get served sooner. But as when many are impatiently waiting their turn in some day-to-day matter, and someone says to his neighbour: "You go now, I can easily wait", everyone becomes more relaxed, the whole atmosphere becomes more friendly, because each realizes he was partly to blame for the strained feeling. Something of this sort should be felt by those waiting before the confessional.

We must realize that, whenever we are in church, we share the presence of Christ in the Eucharist. We have been admitted as honoured guests. His desire is that we should show him that we are his guests, by being present. Another reason, a secondary one, for our being there should be to help to create a certain atmosphere, an atmosphere of love and readiness to help. We enter a church, in fact, not just to see to our own personal affairs, nor with the idea that others are no concern of ours . . . . Even should we have long to wait before our turn comes, the time is not to be wasted; for it is not only a place, but a time, of grace. Even the penance of waiting has its source in grace.

Now comes my turn to confess what I have decided in my preparation. The confession is not to be made in a spirit of rejoicing at the resolutions made or the absolution expected, but in all humility. The reality, indeed, is that I have done this and that, and this is what I am. The confession must show the priest what the sinner really is. It is only too easy, in the consciousness of the resolutions made, to see one's past as something already disowned, and not a part of oneself.

I confess, then, in the tranquillity of truth, without reserve, in unfeigned humility; taking, as it were, a step backwards so as to feel the full weight of guilt that bears on me, yet confessing in a faith that hopes all things. It is true, I have already made my act of contrition and resolutions, and so emerged already, in a way, from the deepest regions of sin; at the same time, it is not for me to grant pardon, but for God. I must go back a step; or it may be that I have to become more humble still through contrition and resolutions and see that my resolutions were, at first, only on the human level, and that only through the grace of absolution, through the counsel given, through the penance acting upon them can they be fully validated sacramentally. I must hope for all things, including the power to keep my resolutions, not from myself, but from the grace of the Lord. In faith will I listen to the counsels of the Spirit, in faith receive absolution, in faith too I now make my confession.

In confessing, we should dwell as little as possible on the circumstances, confining ourselves to the bare sins, to what we have actually done; only in exceptional cases saying: "I do not know whether this was in fact a sin. . . ." We can always, if we think hard enough, find an excuse for most things; but the thing to do is simply to follow our conscience and confess calmly. If something is submitted to absolution which, in fact, did not bear appreciably on the Lord's cross, then so much the better. What is really not to be tolerated is the penitent speaking at length to exonerate himself. Certainly, he should not self-righteously accuse himself of things he knows not to be sins. Nor must he try to invert the rôles and take on the function of the confessor. Too many confess as if they were wholly ignorant of what grace is. The grace of confession is a special, characteristic, unique kind of grace, which only requires of men that they unreservedly admit their sins, in truth (which implies contrition) and in faith. Only in faith can the penitent hear the voice of the Spirit and respond as he ought, that is in the personal manner the Spirit desires. The grace of confession envisages, not sinners in general, but me, and it adapts itself to the sinner in the measure in which he makes his personal response.

We who live under the New Testament dispensation only too easily forget that God is justly wrathful with the sinner, and so we do not realize what his infinite mercy means. His grace and mercy, indeed, always precede any conversion, but yet his pardon insistently awaits the sinner's turning to him. This turning is expressed in a truly contrite confession of sin, which is, therefore, far from being merely a disciplinary ordinance of the Church. It is, in fact, the response to God by which we show we are followers of Christ crucified, the New Testament mode of response. For a sinner so to respond by his confession is itself a great grace; we easily forget that. If we love someone, we try to be what he expects us to be, so that he too may appear as we expect; but with God we make no such attempt, we fail to do our part in that mutual relationship that grace both presupposes and effects. If someone invites a friend to go out with him, he asks him if it suits him, if he has the time, if he is not too tired; he awaits a suitable answer so as to arrange accordingly. God has always something in view for us, and he wants to know, not for the sake of knowing but for us to be open with him, what our situation is. We should, then, in the manner of our disclosure, show ourselves capable of understanding what God intends for us. We can comprehend the Spirit of God only by his response to a confession made in all sincerity. If someone confesses: "In the last two weeks I have sometimes treated my employees badly. That is all", the confessor will know that there is something amiss in this confession, but he has nothing to lay hold of that will enable him to put it right. He will just say a word or two relating to the sin confessed, but with feeling that it is beside the point. The Spirit, which desires to speak through him, does not reach the heart of the penitent by means of his confession.

God has endowed man with a sense of sin, but it can become

blunted. Man no longer troubles about what sin is; he commits it with a sort of good conscience, and does not want it to cause him any inner anxiety. None the less, if others do something wrong, he feels it as such; he only turns away from the sight of his own guilt. Most people have a constant pricking of conscience which points to something of which they are guilty, and that makes them feel the need of purification.

They look, then, if they have no knowledge of confession, for someone or other to tell their faults to, but they never come to an end with their confessing. They go round in circles, and often get so mixed up as to be unable to distinguish the essential from the non-essential, their own deeds from those of others. The one, definite step eludes them.

This step is what confession is. It is the clarification of his situation that brings relief to the sinner. It brings his bewilderment to an end. Yet this clarification is not achieved by him in confessing, but pertains to the Lord, who makes a gift of it to his Church.

Three times did the Lord ask the disciple who had denied him; Simon, lovest thou me? He asked him that as the one against whom the threefold sin had been committed. He could, also, have asked it in the name of God in the Trinity, expressing thereby the community of nature of the three Persons as opposed to the one sinner. His own unity with the Father and the Spirit admits no element of disorder, being communion of the three Persons in unity of nature. The same Son can give himself, equally as the only-begotten Son and as the one who reveals the life of the Trinity.

Peter, the sinner, here attained a clarification of a wholly mysterious nature, which he could never come to grasp. He was questioned, and had to be content with being questioned as the triune God wished. In Peter all of us are comprised who sin and confess. The sacrament is put at our disposal; the confession we make does not follow according to our sole judgment, but must correspond with what we are asked. We have no way of knowing beforehand what this will be. All the scenes enacted between Christ and individual sinners differ. They are directed by him; he puts his finger on one thing or another. He has no rigid procedure, but, with all its variations, he acts always as representing the living God in Trinity. He may insist on the letter, or, discarding it, set store wholly on the Spirit. His treatment of the woman taken in adultery was quite different from his dealing with Thomas, the unbelieving apostle.

Something of this flexible character the Lord gives to sacramental confession, which is thus, within the official framework, an interchange between two persons. The priest hears what is being confessed, but he can interrupt it by putting questions, as it were guiding the flow into a different course. This he does in the Holy Spirit, through whom in every confession the official and the personal element is fused into a unity, a mysterious unity that derives ultimately from that of the Trinity. The penitent sets about his confession as prepared beforehand. He may find, however, that the whole scheme is upset, that the grace questioning him makes him take quite a different perspective, carries him into a region other than he had envisaged. Until the absolution is pronounced, he is still in the state of a penitent confessing, who has not only to speak but also to listen and answer. The course is not controlled by him. It may happen that, in this interchange, he may lose his bearings; in that case, so much the better! What he intended to present as if on a plate, now seems to him quite inappropriate, the whole emphasis has changed, everything must be expressed differently, or else it may seem quite impossible to express in words.

After being absolved, on leaving the confessional, he has

gained an entirely new insight into his sins. It incorporates what he had thought out for himself, but also changed it and gone beyond it. Along with this, he has been given a vivid sense of the Church, in its subjective and objective side, its union of the official and the personal; a new experience too of what the sacraments mean, with their combination of the formal and the informal. It is a great blessing for the sinner to be able to immerse himself in this mysterious gift of God, for he can no more understand and find words to express himself before God than he can understand or express in human terms God himself.

The Confessor's Advice

The right disposition in which to receive the advice of the confessor is one of faith and trust. Once we have made a sincere confession, after due preparation in the light of the Spirit, we can be perfectly certain that the advice given will be precisely what God means for us in particular. Whether it enunciates some general truth or, in the design of the confessor, something adapted to the individual need, makes no difference. Whatever its form, it must be accepted in a childlike faith which takes for granted its rightness and acknowledges its value for the penitent personally, and in a spirit of openness that enables it to take root in the memory. The word I receive is directed to me and binding on me, and, at the same time, binds me to all other penitents; it is drawn out of the one, indivisible storehouse of the divine word. Though addressed to me personally, it should, through me, reach others also, and work its effect on the whole Church. This word I have received should have an enduring, perceptible effect. It is like a seal with which I have been stamped, a stamp of truth others should be able to perceive on me. It is a word which expresses the fact of my election and consequent obligation, a word too which God has specially selected for me from the infinite range of his eternal word to utter to me; though that does not mean its severance from the totality of the divine word. God's whole word is, as it were, a circle and the Church another. The point of contact between the two is the word that I hear, coming from the fulness of God, through me, into the fulness of the Church. The moment I am cleansed, I, despite my sins, am made worthy to represent the Church before God the redeemer. God is never divided, and always has before his eyes the totality of the world to be redeemed; and it is I who am to represent the Church in hearing his word for the world. I am "worthy" of this word through his bearing the burden of the sacrament and acceptance of the responsibility entailed. All this is linked closely to the mystery of the Incarnation. The Son made man became God's representative on earth. He is fully man and remains fully God. As man and the new Adam he bears the bride, the Church, in himself, giving birth to it by his Passion and sending into it his own Spirit.

The penitent is always liable to see the whole process as concerned with him alone and no one else. He has made his own personal confession, and the priest answers him accordingly. But the important thing is for him to pass beyond the immediate personal application and to see the objective side. The effect of the sacrament should be to widen his outlook so that he sees it independently of its own relation to himself, as the Spirit of God at work in the world. In confession, therefore, he ought to try and read into the advice given as much as he possibly can, and this in virtue of the duty implied by the sacrament to encounter, as sinner, the Holy Spirit and receive him. That duty is completely objective, but the sinner always tends to see it subjectively, particularly as regards the advice he receives. Perhaps he thinks; I have heard that a dozen times before, or: He will probably say the same to everyone else. . . . What he should do, on the contrary, is to attend to the objective rightness of what the confessor says; and that can be very difficult.

Further, if the priest says: "We will include everything as God sees it", it is not just an easy way of evading judgment on individual matters. The penitent should take it as an urgent summons to commit, once and for all, his entire self, thoughts and opinions to God's omniscience and judgment, and to live henceforth by this commitment. Even if, after a really serious confession, he is given advice that seems practically meaningless, he must yet say to himself that there too the Holy Spirit is at work. This he must believe because the sacrament belongs to the Spirit. Of course, human stupidity and negligence will often impair its effect and lessen the power of God's word. But, in spite of this, we should persist in seeing even apparently futile advice as proceeding from the fulness of God's power and expressing his truth. The very fact of knowing that it comes from authority should set us at rest, and we ought rather to look to see whether it is not our own dullness that is at fault, and should take for granted the value of the advice.

What the confessor has said to us we must be careful to retain in the memory, so as to direct our course by it. It will then be vividly present when the time of temptation comes, and we can no longer clearly see the insistent demands the sacrament makes on us. It will help us, also, to realize that we are not being guided by some distant God, but by the Holy Spirit, audible to us in the confessional and personally concerned with us. Our confession, though past, continues its efficacy through this enduring element in it, and from it we gain strength to withstand temptation. But if we had listened, at the time, to these same words as embodying merely a general, well known truth, none of their force would have remained in us.

Finally, the confessor imposes a penance. We learn from this two things. The first is that the same God who consoles, advices, encourages us in the word of the Spirit is one who punishes; and that the same who is to be taken back into grace is, in God's eyes and through God, one who makes atonement. The second thing is what we learn from the slightness of the penance, its disproportion with the gravity of sin, namely that it is a penance imposed by the God who bore all sins, God the redeemer. It brings me up suddenly against the fact of the enormous burden God took upon himself for my sake, and that is far more affecting, far more shaming, than the fact of my punishment. This penance is to be accepted in a Christian spirit, in a willingness to carry it out fully without stopping to weigh and assess it. At times, a more severe penance may be imposed, but even so it is always infinitely lenient in comparison with the sins.

If we are given as penance some prayer, as is generally the case, we must bear in mind that it is an act of worship, and that, in saying this prayer once again after being absolved, we are joined in a new fashion to God. As we look on the Passion of the Son, as penance constrains us to do, we are moved to prayer and worship; being penitent is not a passive state, but means we are invited anew to approach God and unite ourselves with him. This action of ours can be described as penance only in an analogous sense. It could equally well be called thanksgiving. It is, however, called penance, because the Lord has himself done penance for us, and has thereby given us a spirit of penance in turning our gaze to the cross. We do not reflect enough on the symbolic character of our penance, but God expects us to realize this, treating us here, as in other connections, as mature persons.

It is part of the Father's joy to form the penitent in such wise that the Son can recognize himself in him. The converse too is sometimes expressed, as by St. John: the Son forms men such that the Father can recognize himself in them. The love of the Father forms us too. The Son demands of us that we imitate him in his attitude as penitent, his stripping himself before the Father; and in so far as the Christian approaches this attitude, it is the Father who forms him. To confess is to present oneself naked before God, and the act forming us is the Father's speaking to us through the Holy Spirit. In requiring our confession the confessor represents the Son; in the words of counsel he gives, he represents the Father and the Spirit. When he elicits from the penitent a positive resolve to live a Christian life in following Christ, he manifests the part played by the Father in the sacrament. It is, indeed, a long way from the act of confessing, in which the sinner shows himself in his true colours, to a complete preparedness to follow Christ. That the Son should bring the penitent to confession is already a great step, but it is due to the act of the Father, in the Holy Spirit, that the Son is revealed to the penitent, and that he is thereby prevented from falling back to the same point where he stood before. God's representative in confession must not content himself with taking cognizanze of what is told him; he must, precisely as representing God, intervene actively in moulding the life of the penitent. He must stir up a renewed desire for purification, not only that effected by absolution, but that which should spring from the act of confessing, of self-manifestation. That is a creative act; it is making something out of nothing, an act of the Father brought about and vivified by the creative Spirit. It is, indeed, the Spirit who, out of a number of weak, scattered resolves, creates a living, integral whole.

Absolution

After the penance has been imposed, there follows the absolution. The penitent has been brought, by what the confessor says to him, to a readiness to atone, to a heart-felt contrition, and then, suddenly, the grace of forgiveness is poured out on him. The penance prescribed makes him see, by its extreme inadequacy, that it is God who has really satisfied for sin. It is a sobering experience, as the examination of conscience was; and it is just what he needs to dispose him for the grace which exceeds all measure.

The sinner is set free from his sins; they have been taken away once and for all. The time for further consideration of his sins is past; they have been expiated, have disappeared, totally ingulfed in the Lord's Passion. It is for us now to look for them within the Passion, and to learn how far we share the blame for the death of Christ. They are now like a memory for which no space can be found within us, since it is all needed to accomodate the immense measure of grace; for this not only fills the existing space, but expands it. The content is greater than the vessel, and our whole existence is taken up into this grace. Christ now lives in us, and his grace, constantly increasing, claims more and more space. It allows no one to share it, but demands all. Up till now we have, as it were, made some faltering attempt to surrender ourselves, but grace now comes to take us. Even if we had counted on receiving absolution, were certain it would be given, yet, when the moment comes, we are taken by surprise; the grace of absolution so much surpasses our expectation. Absolution always makes so great demands that Christ alone can meet them. With it he gives himself so as, in a sense, to satisfy what his own grace demands, knowing that the dwelling we offer is too small for him.

In the light of absolution we come to see why, earlier, excessive preoccupation with our sins was forbidden, why we were required to make a complete break, why we could not unravel all the circumstances of our sins and trace them to their roots. It was no use trying to look at them as if from a distance since that would only confine us within ourselves. On the contrary, the insight gained into our sins, the confession, counsel and penance, should take us out of ourselves, even, in a certain sense, depersonalize us, so as to make way for the personality of Christ that fills all. The process of clearing the way and cutting loose from oneself must not be too long drawn out, so that, when the Lord comes, we may attend to him exclusively.

The person prone to scruples must break off his train of reflections sooner than he feels inclined. He must adhere to the tempo assigned by God to the sacrament; otherwise, while busied with himself, grace passes him by, and he will hear the words of absolution with his attention distracted. Perhaps he was not listening properly at the time when the confessor was giving his counsel, thinking he knew better how his condition was. He needs to be brought to adjust his time to that of God. There is, also, the opposite case, where the penitent has long been ready, and, even before God's absolution has been pronounced, has absolved himself. Here the tempo must be slowed down. The whole sacramental procedure is a clear indication that God knows and takes into consideration our tempo, but also expects we should consider and respect his. Two distinct *tempos* react mutually, and should be made to harmonize, just as husband and wife have to adjust themselves to each other in marriage. The penitent cannot tell God to hurry up and catch up with him, or to go slower because he is not yet ready. What he must do is to fit in with the prescribed timing of the Church in the administration of the sacrament, somewhat as a wife must conform to the imposed timing of travail and birth. The Church decides each stage, and the penitent must obey.

Absolution is given in the name of the Father, of the Son, and of the Holy Ghost. The whole course of the redemption from the Father to the Son to the Spirit, and from the Spirit back to the Son and the Father is expressed in this formula. To exercise his office, the priest possesses the Holy Ghost, whom the Son sent into the sacrament for it to be completed; and the Son, after his Passion, instituted the sacrament in order to fulfil the Father's mission. In this way, everything, from beginning to end, leads back to the fulfilling of theFather's design to redeem the world, and, at the same time, the will of the Trinity is seen at work in each phase of the redemption. The priest has been given the power of the Father, the Son, and the Holy Ghost, the widest and most absolute power, so that there is nothing to query or that requires explanation about the power to absolve. This power expresses the presence of the Trinity in the Church of sinners and saints. The penitent knows that he has been made participator in this unity of the Trinity through his membership of the Church which possesses sacramental confession. The Church which both confesses and absolves is, as it were, carried up into the Trinity, into the sphere of the divine grace imparted to it for the salvation of the world of sin. This sphere is like a space in the Trinity made ready to receive the Church, where reconciliation is being ever granted and incorporation effected into the unity of God.

The penitent finds in absolution a reason for self-abasement; it is God who does everything, and he is powerless. Absolution is the final stage of the humiliation wrought in confession. In the whole process there is never occasion for self-glorification, but only for glorifying God in his Trinity, who, in the Son, condescended to our level.

Penance

The penance we perform is both an end and a beginning. It is imposed as a punishment for the past, but performed in virtue of a new disposition. This throws a new light on the character of the penance. Since it is so slight in itself, merely symbolic, it must, at least, be taken for what it is, namely prayer. The Lord prescribed confession so that we should attain redemption, but being redeemed means that we seek anew the way to God, stand in a new attitude of prayer before him. This is what the penance should effect in us. It is not only an external act, but one that should form us interiorly and bring us nearer to God, a seed producing new fruit. While we are intent on performing a penance, new seed is already being sown. We only notice that when we have begun to pray. We perceive, then, how infinitesimally slight is the penitential character of this prayer, and so we associate ourselves with what the Lord has done all alone on our behalf. None the less, it is a prescribed penance, and we ought to accept it, as much as possible, in a penitential spirit. Then it will be a source of grace, carrying over uninterruptedly the grace of absolution into the grace of everyday life.

The penance, though fixed, is, in a sense, free in that it is open to us to prolong and extend it, as we see fit. We can look on what has been imposed as being merely a minimum to which we can add, and ask God to condescend to accept this addition and apply it as he will. In doing this, we show we understand that grace is always susceptible of increase, and that we are ready for what the new measure of grace bestowed by God through confession may demand of us.

To sum up, here are a few practical considerations. What is of primary importance in confession is to look to God rather than to ourselves, to be fully aware that God is listening to us, and therefore to speak in the way we know he wants to hear us. Our whole endeavour must be to give God the glory. We think back on our former confessions and consider in what ways we have again departed from our resolutions and been untrue to our lights. Or perhaps our last confessions were defective in some way, merely a formal catalogue of sins. We look into them with an eye open to signs of the indifference and lukewarmness that was our disposition at the time. In this present confession we try to be ourselves once more, more like what God, in his love, intended us to be. Our aim is, in this preparation now, to lay the foundations of a new life.

What sort of a preparation did we make last time? Did we have, then and on previous occasions, insufficient time or desire to go into the matter thoroughly? Did we just hurriedly think up one or two things that we thought should be confessed, without being properly contrite? Real contrition is not compatible with volatility; it must be allowed time to grow and develop. Should we know in advance that we will not have much time on the day, we ought to try and settle everything, more or less, beforehand.

In examining our conscience, we should distinguish between isolated acts and a settled attitude. If we confess we have sinned against the truth, the question is what that means, whether we have told a deliberate lie two or three times or more, or whether we live in a permanent disposition to use evasion and lies whenever it suits us in our relations with God and men. Even at this very moment, in formulating our confession, we may catch ourselves out in falsehood, choosing expressions that conceal, rather than disclose, the reality.

Further, we should ask ourselves if we really confess sins as such, that is as things we have to get rid of, and not simply as facts and occurrences we perceive and regret; whether, in fact, our disposition is one that is seriously concerned with expiating these faults, and forming resolutions to that end. The purpose of amendment should not consist merely in the knowledge of certain procedures which we hope will suffice to overcome our failings. It must spring from unreserved openness to God and the Church, which is the true penitential attitude, and we have to see that something of this openness continues later, when it comes to carrying out the resolutions.

It is a good thing, at least occasionally, to take the New Testament as a standard by which to judge ourselves; it provides something much more realistic than a systematic list of possible sins. How do we measure up to what Christ, the Incarnate Son of God, expects of us? It is easier to grasp sin as an outrage to Christ crucified than as an offence against the Supreme Good. We might dwell on some of the sayings of the Lord, or read one or two of St. Paul's exhortations to his communities; or else imagine our Lord taking his apostles apart and explaining his teaching, or reproaching them and, in a way, taking on the function of their confessor. What does he hold most important, and emphasize more than anything else? We confess, not as isolated individuals, but in communion with the apostles admonished and "confessed" by the Lord. Or we can take one of the parables, say that of the king making his reckoning with his servant. That is what the kingdom of heaven is, the meeting of the king with his servant and their liberation from sin. Or take a passage like "How hard it is for a rich man to enter the kingdom of heaven!"; and see how we cling to our sins, as reluctant to be parted from them as a rich man from his gold. Everywhere Scripture presents us with a standard to judge by, exhibits the true relationship between God and man. Everywhere in it is something that touches us personally and places us in the original Christian setting, the only true one. Everywhere we find ourselves invited, prepared, induced to make our confession. We are always being told nowadays to read the Bible more. For what purpose? In what frame of mind? Undoubtedly, so as to become as God's revealed word would have us.

If we feel we make no progress with our confessions, and always have the same faults, we should, on occasion, take pains to find out just what our own special problem is. Not to be satisfied with a mere general regret or vague feeling of hopelessness. Rather we must believe for certain that help is at hand. Suppose I am always catching myself telling lies, great or small. What is the reason? Convenience? Vainglory? Fear of exposure? Vindication of my own worth? Delight in putting others in the shade? A real effort must be made to investigate the basic attitudes and motives and face them squarely.

Perhaps we have confessed properly, but paid little attention to what the confessor said, convinced that we really know better and have no need of advice. What the confessor says is the same as he has been saying for weeks and years, and, if it has served no purpose all that time, neither will it now. We fail to hear the word as what it truly is, the constantly repeated admonition of the Holy Ghost; we know already the lesson and its uselessness for us. It is high time, then, for us to admit that, up to now, we have never heard the word properly. We consider we have done enough in speaking to God about our sins, and never once realize that, in this dialogue, what God says to us is far more important and effectual.

9. CONFESSION AS IT AFFECTS OUR WAY OF LIFE

The New Man

OUR RELATIONSHIP with God after absolution is seen to be quite different from before. We are set free from our bondage, and, in this state of freedom, we stand before God in quite a different fashion from when we were in the state of sin. No longer are we estranged from God, for our attitude to him is now determined by love and reverence.

God is eternal in his trinitarian life, and man is transient. In absolution, God breathes into man something of his eternity. The freedom man receives has its source in the eternal love, which empowers him to love anew, both more freely and in a more absolute fashion, as the outcome of his state of wholeness. It is a state in which he belongs to God, which has been formed by God, maintained by God and, if necessary, purified again by God. In this state everything is endowed with a splendour that derives from the life which is eternal.

Should one fall again into sin, the estrangement from God makes itself known in a feeling of apprehension; all kinds of things then interpose themselves between the sinner and God. During this interval between one confession and the next, the sinner may experience many things that separate him from God, diminish his freedom, obstruct his faith, cloud his view of eternal life. Absolution restores this view for the person who is ready to kneel before God in contrition and acknowledgement of sin. Then God's eternal goodness, mercy and love are opened up again for the sinner, sent out, as it were, to meet him and bring him home.

From there he returns to ordinary life. At the time he made the effort to confess rightly, he saw his life and circumstances in a new light. Now he goes to work with a fresh hope, a hope that bears the stamp of the absolution received. He has been given to share actively in the interchange of love between the three divine Persons, and the question is how this love is to be put into practice. This state of purity and love is, in fact, indicated by its effects. If he keeps this love jealously to himself, on the ground that it is given to him alone, it will soon wither away. But if he is aware of its secret, that it wills to be used in the service of others, then it will remain in him in full vigour. It is a treasure that remains intact only by being spent with utter recklessness; then love preserves its pristine power as a miracle wrought by absolution, and then it becomes a miracle constantly repeated. Once the chains of sin are broken, those of grace begin to be forged; and though the occasions of sin are many, one leading to another, those of grace are far more numerous.

While the Son was living among men, he saw how much was needed in order that God's word should become firmly rooted. He showed this in the parable of the sower, where we see how many conditions must be fulfilled for the seed to grow. He saw what little effect his similitude had on his disciples who heard it. The word he spoke was ineffectual to make his hearers into good soil or to compel them to prepare the ground for it.

So from the ideas expressed in the parable he went on to

institute the sacraments. They all have an absolute character; they produce an absolute effect, something integral and perfect which springs from God and, being divine, cannot be surpassed. It is possible he might have framed confession in such a way that only what we find most difficult to bear in sin should be taken away, and man would be left with part of his previous life, of his past sins, and enlightened as to his future. Instead, the sacrament is a completely new beginning, a divine forgiveness that takes away everything. The person who sins again after confession does not add something to what was already there, but begins again with sin. Yet – and this is the essential point – he began before that with a state of sinlessness. If he reflects on what was given him at the moment of absolution for the coming period, he will see that he had been made into good soil, that all the burden he bore had been removed, that his soul had been restored to innocence; and only his indolence and indifference, or perhaps his attachment to sin, has made him once more a sinner.

Confession and absolution bring about the best dispositions for gaining indulgences, when one is freed from sin and intimately united with Christ, and so can easily enter into the intentions of the Church and fulfil what it prescribes.

Sin, its circumstances and effects, are sometimes a subject of discussion on a purely secular level; and when it is a matter of one's own sins, they are generally somewhat embellished. Perhaps they are related as a form of entertainment, or else to throw light on something else, or to make one seem somehow important, occasionally too to get them off one's chest. Whether consciously or not, the reaction of the listener is awaited, and the gravity of the sin estimated accordingly; or else it is simply contrasted with one's own judgment. Such a discussion may also be held in order to put an end to one's own interior dialogue with sin, of which it is hard to say whether it is, in fact, a dialogue at all or just a monologue.

Christian confession, on the contrary, precludes embellishment, comparisons, the testing of another's reaction, for the sacrament is something objective. The penitent may prepare what he is to confess, decide its precise formulation and even the tone of voice and the significant pauses. He may learn it by heart; and yet it will have quite a different sound when he says it, for it is now conveyed by the confessor to God, as the response to a demand on his part. It is now incorporated into the framework of unchangeable laws which have long been part of the Church's tradition and practice, and which give sin its objective character. Sin is there present, as was that of our first parents in paradise, clearly seen for what it is, with nothing to palliate it, independent of man's judgment, its ultimate effects unforeseeable. This creates a new relationship between penitent and confessor, which itself defies comprehension, being, so to speak, the echo of a definite relationship between God and the sinner. God's relationship to the confessor is one he has himself determined, and which is indicated, once and for all, by the cross. The sinner stands at a focal point which lies within him and yet is not brought into being through his sole agency; and it, in turn, casts its rays on a number of objects impossible to count. It is a focus to which stream, as so many rays, all his past deeds, their circumstances and motives; and yet these cannot be used to determine it on psychological grounds, since everywhere grace is at work invisibly with its alteration of values. Consequently, the sinner cannot know where he really stands. The light of grace, already shed over his whole past, and now, in confession, made evident to the sinner, has deprived him of the last standard of judgment he possessed. On the one hand, his whole past appeared to him in this light as a dead weight, but, when he came to draw conclusions from it, there appeared the light of grace itself, desirous of absolving him, but yet, in his preparation for confession, almost seeming oppressive, because of its insistence on the absolute necessity of confession. It demands imperatively that the sinner take the way of grace. There is no question now of his losing himself in his past, for this now exists only as something that demands to be confessed.

This demands brings the sinner face to face with the truth. Till then, in view of his past, he thought he knew the kind of person he was. Now, however, he is given a new aspect, and that not merely in his own eyes, but one which precludes his recognition on the part of his associates and any resumption of his former relationship and occupations, in fact, all that might have influenced his future course. The qualities which are now mine are, in each case, other than those I had before. I can accept that I can no longer recognize myself; but the really difficult thing about confession is that others should no longer recognize me, that they are bound to conclude that I had been living among them till now under a mask, and continue to look for me beneath it, because it seemed to have grown into me, whereas I have to show them my real self, that of one redeemed and converted. I am freed from the entanglement of sin, but that only puts me in the awkward position of being a different person from what everyone thought; besides, how is it going to be possible for me, a sinner, to live henceforth as a child of grace? If only everything about me were new, that I could go to a foreign country where I was quite unknown! But this favour is not granted me; I have to stay where I am. Only, now St. Paul's words must be true of me: "No longer I live, but Christ lives in me", words which have been awaiting me these two thousand years. Is it possible my confession was a colossal mistake, since it seems to have upset everything? But it was not I who initiated the upheaval; it was the word of the Lord spoken by his representative, the priest. This word seized on me and the whole confessing Church, from which it goes out over the world around us; and the world either shakes its head in unbelief or else, by slow degrees, approaches faith.

Confession and Everyday Life

The events of ordinary life make our moods vary from one extreme to another. When we meet with success, our spirits are raised. We are joyful on feast-days, though they may concern us personally only slightly apart from their being feasts, and, all at once, we meet with some unpleasant experience and become depressed. The sacraments of the Church, however, offer us the possibility of escape from these constant fluctuations and of attaining a consistent disposition. Of course, a good confession will bring about extreme changes of mood, from horror at the gravity of our sins to joy at being absolved; but these moods are intimately connected, there is a definite point where they are capable of being integrated. This point is the penitential attitude, an infused gift of the Lord, and at the same time, something he exacts of us. It is an attitude of openness before him, of awareness that he sees all our actions, but as one ready to help, to intervene and to bestow his grace. This is not a matter of a mood which comes and goes, but of a firm and fortifying disposition grounded on the fact of redemption. Once we have been secured, through the practice of confession, in this disposition, it is within our power to live accordingly, to attune our various sentiments and attitudes to it, and, as penitents in God's presence, to remain always open to his grace.

In ordinary everyday life everything that happens will be

entirely different from confession, yet each thing can be related to it. It would be quite out of order to leave the confessional with a sense of liberation and being cleansed, and then, quite unconcernedly, to expose oneself to fresh occasions of sin, as if with a perfect right to be upheld by the grace received, on the presumption that God would come to seek us once more, at best before we fell into sin, at the very worst afterwards.

Our conception of the sacrament must not be one that reduces it to the single element of absolution, for this would result in confession weakening, rather than strengthening, our interior disposition. It would, then, bring about a certain indifference to sin, and cause us to adopt a warped interpretation of the maxim *ama et fac quod vis,* reserving to oneself the *fac quod vis* and consigning the *ama* to God as one who will always forgive us, whatever we do. Confession is an obligation we owe to the cross. It comes from the cross, and leads back to it. For that reason, it both demands and effects a disposition analogous to that of the Lord himself.

The Lord also comes from the cross and goes to the cross. He comes with the intention of going to the cross. In the beginning of the world God the creator separated the elements, above and beneath, left and right; and there already the Son saw a sign of the cross to come. The Father separated them and established order among them. Man, in sinning, separated himself from God, distinguished good and evil, and replaced God's order by the disorder of chaos. The Son on the cross restores the division intended by the Father, and, in establishing it, he passes judgment. He brings back good and evil into unity by doing the good and suffering the evil. By separating them he draws them into the unity of the redemption; and when he has drawn everything into his death, he descends to the place of the Father's justice, and surveys the Father's work and, at the same time, his own work of separating sin and sinner. There he leaves behind him, once and for all, certain things with which, after his resurrection, he desired no further relationship, to which we also have no further relationship. There is a parallel to this in the time after confession. The things which the Son relinquished in his journey through hell should, by the inherent logic of confession, be made inaccessible to us also. They become so, if we continue in our disposition as penitents. What confession settles is finished once and for all; and that means, once again, living in view of the cross.

After each confession, we ought to live with a view to the next, which should be still more comprehensive in scope, still more inclusive of the world and its sins. Each succeeding confession should take on increasingly the dimensions of the Church. We ought to feel that, up to that time, we have been too individualistic in our confessions, that, while borne along by the confessions of others, we have not taken enough share in theirs. The Church, which takes on its shoulders the confessions of all, and always keeps in mind the cross of its Lord, should, more and more, serve as our model in confession.

Confession should be a real, active element in the life of the Christian, not merely a formality. It should be a significant part in the sinner's intercourse with God, in which he receives forgiveness and participates in the single great grace of pardon; for pardon not only removes guilt, but contributes something positive to future living. If our confessions are of this kind, something of them is bound to flow out into our everyday life, influencing it at every moment, whether we are conscious of it or not, and not merely at times of stress or temptation. One and the same sacrament adapting itself to all kinds of situations shows the Christian how diverse are the ways the Lord uses to make contact with him, ways along which the Lord wills us to accompany him in his sacrament of redemption. In every circumstance, he shows himself as the living Lord, pointing the way, commanding, listening, admonishing and comforting, binding to himself and, at the same time, setting free, taking on himself what is ours and giving what is his. All these forms of encounter should be continuously effective by being separately experienced and developed while always keeping their relationship to the one sacrament. Through the sacrament, we are constantly shown new, unsuspected ways of living in Christ.

This diversity of modes of life reacts on the sacrament itself, if we use it properly, causing it to reveal new aspects and how it acts in the penitent's everyday life to fortify his interior disposition and give it wider scope. In every instance, he is shown what has been made possible through the sacrament, and, on the other hand, what has been definitely achieved by its means and so comes no more into question. In preparing for confession, he may have used Scripture and meditation, but he must find a place for them also in his ordinary life. In that way, in preparing for confession, he will not have to strain his memory unduly, or probe far into the future; his constant contact with the Lord and his revelation in Scripture will make his examination of conscience both easy and profitable. Christ is the mirror of the Christian; and if he is accustomed to look in it every day, he will, when he comes to examine himself, soon see himself as he is.

The grace of confession also enables us to treat others more generously; it makes us want them to share in it, and look for ways to help them to do so, while avoiding any kind of misplaced zeal. Those of us who have no outward apostolic mission must remember that we all have an interior vocation to prayer, which has an apostolic effect. This we have to cultivate, and, at the same time, so conduct ourselves towards our fellowmen as to make the faith attractive to them. All that the Christian does and accepts can be productive of good, even though this may not be capable of being exactly expressed. He will look on others, not as sinners irretrievably lost, but, if they are Catholics, as open to receive the grace of absolution. Those who are not Catholics present greater difficulty, since they are strangers to the grace of confession. We come across so many who are totally enclosed in their egoism, their petty concerns, but yet we cannot tell if they will not soon be steeped in the grace of absolution. The question is, what can we do to help them to a knowledge of this, to open their eyes?

Many experience a strong repugnance to confession, but, once they have been, they realize it was not so difficult after all. They were carried along by an imperceptible grace. All at once they realize something of what the Church's prayer means; they feel themselves supported by the prayer of many people they do not know, possibly also that of some particular person. That brings them to see they too have a duty to pray. Although each confession is conducted in perfect secrecy, there is yet an immense scope in it for the prayer of others, who participate in it without knowing anything of the details, of all those who are content to put their prayers at the disposition of others without curiosity as to the outcome. This power of prayer is a clear indication of the discretion with which the Lord treats our sins. Confession takes place in the setting of the Church as a whole; all its members are involved and may realize it, yet they neither know, nor wish to know, what goes on between the sinner and Christ. In many cases, we help one another by what we say; but even then we are most helpful when we are content to remain in ignorance. Two people may be very close; they go together to confession, each without knowing what the other has on his conscience. In spite, however, of the secrecy of confession, they will yet be more closely united through confession, since they have both received the like grace and have gone the same way. Perhaps one of them tells the other that he was impatient with him on one occasion, and was going to confess it; but the latter should not dwell on this, but put it out of his mind at once, as no concern of his. Still, he will pray as much as possible for the other's confession. Their relationship is neither heightened nor impaired through knowing or not knowing their individual sins; nor must either ever ask the other if his confession was assisted by his prayer. Everything to do with confession remains hidden in the mystery of the communion of saints.

Confession and Mission

Confession, together with the prayer that goes with it, enables us, not only, through the grace of Christ, to efface our own sins, but to come to the help of others. Once we realize this, it becomes clear that there is a point where confession and mission meet, and even coincide. The Son's mission is a divine one in its entirety. Even as man he discharges it in a divine manner, abiding, all his life, in an attitude of complete openness before the Father and the Spirit. This is his penitential disposition, in virtue of which he is always able to fulfil the will of the Father in the Holy Spirit, to discharge his mission in an absolutely personal way, and yet with the utmost obedience. His attitude of openness and his conduct form a perfect unity. Even on the cross, where he no longer feels the Father's presence, but bears our sins in suffering, where he enacts for all not merely a general, abstract redemption, but confession in the concrete, confession and mission are at their apex. He fulfils the severest part of his mission, his death on the cross, in the most absolutely open disposition of penitence. And since all varieties of mission start out from the cross, they do so also from his attitude and act of confession.

It may well happen to a person of exceptional holiness, who either has never sinned grievously or has long broken with sin, to see sin as something quite apart, to see it only in its relation with the cross of Christ. He himself, by a special grace, is quite outside the realm of sin. The sins of those with whom he comes in contact are felt as a disturbing element in his intercourse with God, but not as a serious obstacle to it. Yet that is not really the case at all. In contemplating the cross, he will come to experience, from its effect there, the full force with which it ravages the world of men, and so realize that his whole mission is to bring help to sinners.

Perhaps he was himself once a sinner, and, in consequence, always looks on himself as one. In that case, his union with the Lord will be experienced under the form of the grace of confession brought to fulfilment; whether, like St. Mary Magdalen, he encounters the Lord directly, or through the Church by confession and conversion. With him, also, confession will be seen as inseparable from his mission. Even if that particular confession marks a climax in his life, he will try to keep the experience always in being, though in an altered form, not, indeed, for the sake of prolonging the feeling of it, but in order to assimilate himself, as far as he may, to Christ on the cross, and to let himself be sent on behalf of sinners; he was himself formerly one of them, and still reckons himself one. For all others who have a mission which they strive to discharge, confession can serve to reanimate their consciousness of being sent, a compass which points the direction to follow and makes their precise path clear. It is a sign guiding them on their precipitous journey, with all its attendant dangers.

Once a person realizes his mission is to be an intermediary, a channel of grace for others, he will see that each confession he makes ought to add to his fitness for this. The sacrament's importance for him is that it frees him from all that is extraneous to his mission, extends his range, makes him more receptive. If he is dedicated to his mission and desires to live for it alone, he will ardently long to fulfil it according to the will of God. Both elements in it, represented in the sacrament, he will try to satisfy as perfectly as possible, that which concerns him directly, namely receiving for the sake of the other, that which affects the rest of men, namely transmitting what he receives, with ever greater purity. He will go to confession so as to purify himself afresh for his office, to see with clearer vision what belongs to the essence of his mission, and to hand on to others what he receives in confession with the least possible diminution.

There is no mission where the penitential disposition is not of decisive importance, and no sacrament emphasizes so clearly as that of confession how receptive to grace we must be for the sake of our mission. All that impedes its flow must be dissolved and eliminated, so that its free passage may be assured again. Yet we should not hanker after the sacrament on the mistaken view that confession is everything, or desire to confess daily in order to grow to the full stature of our mission. God did not make the sacraments the only source of grace; he gives it also in answer to prayer, and, in addition, we constantly receive further purification and assistance through belonging to the Church. While the communion of saints is, in a certain measure, fostered and sustained by those with a mission to perform, they, in turn, are supported by it, being, as it were, carried along and urged forward by its needs. Besides, the sacraments continue to be operative after their reception. Their action is not absolutely comparable with that of food in the body, which sustains it only for a certain length of time. We should try to draw strength not only from the sacraments, but from the grace given in view of our particular function. On occasion, we may confess before some arduous undertaking, so as to be wholly purified for the purpose, but not always before each successive duty. That would be to overlook the continuous efficacy of the sacrament, and also the freedom of God's grace. Confession is not meant to train us to a state of dependence and keep us immature; on the contrary we should grow up, through it, in such a way that our obedience becomes more and more delicate through a finer sense of what is demanded of us.

There are, also, missions of a less pronounced character, and these often become clear through confession. Confession, in such cases, is a kind of initiation. The confessor perceives the presence of something that calls for cultivation and growth, and so brings it to the fore in confession. The penitent, for his part, comes to sense how confession makes it take on a definite form and character.

Confession and Prayer

The Son always stood before the Father as a penitent, and, consequently, our intercourse with the Lord, whatever its nature, always gives us some share in this disposition of his. What it brings may be something closely related to sacramental confession, but may seem remote from it, and only on closer examination seen to be so connected. Whenever we apply ourselves in faith to the Lord, whatever the manner of our so doing, we are in the sphere of prayer. No believer can apply his mind to Christ in a manner inimical to prayer, as for instance, in such a purely scientific or historical way as to rule out prayer altogether; in fact, this kind of approach would serve, rather, to broaden out his prayer and stimulate it. Prayer in its pure state is a participation in the dialogue of the Lord with the Father in the Holy Ghost, in the dialogue of the Trinity with the world and ourselves. The trinitarian dialogue is all-comprehensive, and our participation is limited to what comes, in some way, within our understanding, such as the sayings of Christ when on earth, his relationship to the Church, the institution of the sacraments, the commandments and counsels. In prayer, it is not always necessary to distinguish the object clearly. We can, on the one hand, pray in view of confession, preparing for it or saying the penance; here the connection is evident. Or else we can choose confession as the subject of prayer, with a view to a better use of the sacrament, for instance. But we can also simply pray without any conscious reference to confession; and yet the connection will be there, since every prayer, if a true one, brings us closer to the Lord's own disposition and imparts something of it.

Christ's disposition is, in itself, simple, but, to our understanding, complex, because it can be looked at from a variety of standpoints. Always, however, we are led to its centre, which is his openness before the Father for the redemption of the world. Consequently, each prayer we utter and that enriches the treasury of the Church takes us further into his disposition, and bears upon the redemption of the world. That is why it is so closely connected with confession. This main characteristic of all prayer also explains why the Church allows so many different forms of prayer and services, so that each person can choose what suits him. If this were not the case, we should have to pray according to a precise system, apportioning their exact share to each beneficiary, the souls in purgatory, penitents, communicants, the missions, and so on. Once we really understand the essential element of prayer, it is an excellent thing to leave our prayer at God's free disposal, whatever the form we choose or the intention we have in mind. Christian prayer ultimately means that the person praying is inserted into the Father's will, just as the Son fulfilled it in each of his acts.

God, being omniscient, knows already what we confess to the priest. As we make every effort to say exactly what the truth is, we come to realize more clearly God's omniscience. When we pray, we should be conscious that God knows what our needs are, if it is a question of petitions; and that he knows in what way we can worship him, if it is that kind of prayer we are offering. This consciousness of ours should not remain purely theoretical, but incite und help us to come before God in utter nakedness, to pray to him in such openness as excludes any reservation, and, where there might be such, seeks to uncover what is hidden. This openness is part of the penitential disposition which goes further and includes "disponibility" to God, a movement towards him in anticipation of what is his will for us. Acknowledgement of sin alone would be insufficient, if we felt we had thereby made satisfaction and could creep back into our shell. The act of confessing implies a movement toward God and submission to his will. The same is true of prayer; it is not only something uttered to God, but also, even more, hearing his word and being prepared to follow it. Prayer is not a monologue but a dialogue; not only the expression of human needs and thoughts, but also laying oneself open for all that God says and requires.

Furthermore, it is the will of the Lord that the penitent should let his confession carry over beyond the actual moment, should be living and effectual in all the time that follows. Likewise with prayer; even when not actually praying, we should carry over our prayer-time into our life. Prayer ought to gather up and express our whole life with all that happens in it. It should be the warrant of our abiding in God. From one confession to the next changes occur in the penitent that are, perhaps, more noticeable to the confessor than to him; and so also from one prayer-period to the next there is development of some kind, since the believer's life is never static, any more than the Son ever halted in his course from the Father back to him. The man who prays, like the penitent, is a follower of the Son, is taken up with him in his going to the Father, which always includes his coming from the Father. Our whole life, in its unity of the two attitudes, of prayer and penitence, reproduces the unity of the Son's own chosen attitude.

Confession and prayer have this in common, that each expresses particular questions, problems, difficulties met with in life. Both of them clearly indicate that the Christian is still in the state where he needs the help of God and the Church, that he cannot emerge from it on his own; but confession does so mainly after fall into sin, prayer more before such a fall. Confession is more a remedy, prayer more a prophylactic. But a state of sin and liability to a future fall are not mutually exclusive; both states are so closely associated in the believer that they equally belong to the spheres of prayer and of confession. One may well confess because faced with a great temptation, and it is open to anyone to pray when he has sinned.

10. THE OFFICE OF CONFESSOR

Preparation

THE RIGHT motives for becoming a priest are all contained in God, they derive fundamentally from Christ's own decision to become man. This decision was reflected even in the priesthood of the Old Testament, and then, after the Incarnation had become a fact, was represented in a wholly new way in the New Testament. Jesus Christ is the priest pure and simple, who goes in search of the souls of all and brings them home to the Father. When his followers decide to become priests, their motives can be as various as are men themselves; yet these motives are all one in Christ. His priesthood, indeed, is a unity of manifold aspects and motives, all of them incorporated by the Father into his priesthood. Each man who decides on this office in following the Son may make a certain choice out of all these, and his preference is quite legitimate, provided that, with it, he also wills the rest.

This choice is influenced particularly by the idea of the sacraments and their administration by the priest. There are many who see in the sacrament of penance the most direct way to influence the sinner and free him for the service of God.

Here the desire to help one's neighbour in Christian charity can find its outlet and operate most effectively. The priest in the course of his training will look on this sacrament as offering the most varied and effective means for pastoral work. While still in the seminary, he reflects on all he may be able to achieve in the confessional. He sees confession more in its sacramental and official character, and prepares himself for his future ministry by prayer and study.

It is not sufficient, however, for him to have an exact knowledge of the sacrament and of the rules laid down by the Church for its administration. What is required, above all, is a complete personal commitment that goes beyond a mere intellectual approach. He has to learn to live in a sacramental setting, to realize he has been placed in a situation analogous to that of the Son sent by the Father. Both the life of the Son in heaven from his decision to take human nature and his whole life on earth up to the cross can be looked on as a preparation for the institution of this sacrament. In view of this, it is easy to realize that the demands made by the Church, indeed by the Son himself, on the confessor are so far-reaching as to embrace his whole life as a priest. At the same time, they are perfectly precise, so that, if this one sacrament takes possession of his whole life, that does not preclude the simultaneous claims of the other sacraments. But it can be considered the foundation from which the whole structure rises.

In heaven the Son prepared to found the sacrament of penance as man. He did so in virtue of his complete acceptance of the Father's will, applying to its execution all his will and faculties, and, at the same time, made everything converge on his divine and human priesthood, on the redemption and absolution of sinners. The same applies to the priest of the New Testament, whom the confessional makes a mediator, like Christ, between heaven and earth. Once he realizes how he continues the work of Christ in virtue of his office, he will see how all he has learnt of the Son, obedience, love, zeal for the Father's glory, absolute devotion to others, must be reproduced in all his life as a priest. No part of it can be subtracted from service to God and man, since the Son sacrificed all to his priesthood. The priest may not view his own sins with indulgence, for the Son was himself without sin. He must strive after a perfection that has its foundation in the sacrament, and will bear a constant responsibility in this regard, both to the Father and to his fellowmen. To be able to do this, he must learn to see both the divine holiness and human sin in a new light, that of the Son giving himself for sinners. In looking on the Son, in his prayer and contemplation, he will, at the same time, always keep in mind the sins of man, seeing both in the light of his function as mediator. Even when he contemplates the life of the Trinity, it will always be with a view to draw some kind of fruit for sinners; and when he meets with sin, he should not stop at the thought of penance and absolution, but go on to envisage how he can present to the penitent sinner (he himself being always one) the image of the self-giving mediator.

When a layman sins, his sin, which is not to be extenuated, is yet "his affair", which he himself has to settle. But if he is going to be a priest and a confessor, the situation is quite different, since he is to be the minister of a sacrament, and, therefore, set in quite a different relationship with other men. When he confesses now, he must do so with a view to his subsequent rôle as confessor, to the purity, self-giving, the priestly form of charity, which he will need then, and in which he now has the duty of initiating himself. When the future priest confesses, he is one of the community of sinners, and this fact too he must understand in its Christian and sacerdotal aspect. He has to see his fellow-sinners and penitents, not only as a theologian, but as one bound to them in the community of the redeemed and the fallen. He must look on them, not with mere human tolerance, but with the eyes of Christ himself, in whose place he, though a sinner, will have to perform the office of pardoning in love. In his contacts with men of all kinds – in the house, the street, the Church – he must foreshadow his future attitude as confessor by the love he shows them, his readiness to give himself, and this without any kind of unctuousness or importunity. Seed is thus sown beforehand which cannot, for the moment, grow, but yet has to be sown long before ordination and the receipt of jurisdiction.

What holds good for the confession of the ordinary Christian applies even more to his, since his desire for the priesthood is reflected in his confession. In confessing, the candidate for the priesthood bears in mind that he too will one day hear confessions. He must, therefore, be careful to omit nothing, and be strict about his own sins, paying particular attention to the matter of fraternal charity and compassion for others. He should also be conscious that the grace he hopes to gain comes from the same store from which he will later impart grace. In all the different parts of confession he ought to be aware of his being in communion with his future penitents; and this demands of him a specially conscious attitude of penitence. For their sake, he should make himself more and more amenable to the working of grace. In practice, this will be shown in his struggle against his defects, in the candour with which he sees himself, in his openness before God, his contrition, his humility in listening to the confessor's advice, his joy in being absolved, the strength he derives from the sacrament. He must yield himself up to be formed anew by the hands of his confessor and in the power of the sacrament, so as to approach more closely the image of the Son, and thereby enabled to form other penitents. Even if he cannot register any definite progress from one confession to the next, he will never relax his will to give himself, always striving for the unattainable ideal of perfect resemblance to Christ. His whole life will be a continuous pursuit of that end. The perfection of the Son of God is like a powerful current, and the most he can hope for is to keep himself within it, and never to escape from it into some quiet corner away from its swirling. In this way, he will come to experience what it means to "live, not I, but Christ in me", realizing it ever anew, more particularly in his situation as penitent and as confessor.

Those who are, later on, to hear confessions themselves should make the words spoken to them by their confessor lead them to a more intimate union with the Spirit. They should accept his counsel as coming from the Spirit, and, in that way, learn what is required to make the counsel they will give accepted likewise. The most important requirement is for the penitent to subject himself in all humility to the confessor's words, and this will result, in part, from the very fact of their spiritual content. In addition, he will try to keep the counsel given always present to his mind, until it has been carried out in practice or superseded by fresh advice. In this, he will also conduct himself as an ordinary Christian, and so gain experience that will serve for his own penitents; in all these ways, he will come to be initiated into a spiritual conception of his future office. His own personal life and effort ought to flow from his relationships with his confessor and the Spirit speaking through him.

Here too is where the Church imitates the life of the Son in the Trinity. The decree of the Incarnation issued from a dialogue between the Father and Son in the Holy Spirit, and the sacrament, founded by the Son and animated by the Spirit, is an active reproduction of this dialogue. Through the counsel he receives the penitent participates in the contact of the confessor with the Holy Spirit, who testifies to what the Father and Son uttered in their dialogue concerning the redemption; and this is made possible only because the incarnate Son, in his attitude of penitence, held himself at the disposal of the Father and the Spirit as regards his mission. The rôles seem to be interchanged, but it is, in fact, the Son who founded the sacrament of penance by placing in it his own Spirit of sonship, and, in that way, the reception of the sacrament always involves imitation of the Son, obedience in his obedience. The Incarnation does not bring the trinitarian dialogue wholly within our understanding, and so our sacramental participation in it has more aspects than we can grasp, which brings out the character of confession as a supernatural source of life. We can never participate in the life of the Trinity in an exterior fashion, without personal involvement, but only by entering on a form of Christian dialogue worthy of such participation. And what form could there be more appropriate than that instituted by the Son, between penitent and confessor, between sinner and divine redeemer in the Church? Further, when the penitent himself is a future confessor, it is even more important for him to grasp the trinitarian character of the dialogue, to understand also all the various standpoints and their inversions when the same man changes from penitent to confessor. It is this change of rôles that brings out the official, hierarchical aspect more clearly, since it is not accountable on purely human grounds, but presupposes and manifests some higher source and foundation.

Hearing Confessions

The priest newly ordained may either welcome the prospect of hearing confessions, as fulfilling a long desire to help his penitents, or else view with alarm so momentous a function, feeling himself inadequate to probe the souls of others; in either case, his first experience will make a strong impression on him. The first time he gives absolution, he is bound to have the feeling of being overwhelmed as if by the flood of grace, so great is the disparity between him, only just ordained, and the tremendous gift of God. He speaks the words he has learned by heart, correctly enough, but will surely feel that the Spirit must have required something more of him, that he should have spoken differently both in matter and in manner, and, in pronouncing absolution, feel lost and bewildered at the power entrusted to him.

As time goes on, he will become inured to this, and then the real danger begins. As long as this feeling of inadequacy persists, he will continue to struggle to give of his best, to let the grace of hearing confessions guide his own life. Habit, however, blunts his zeal. Sitting in the confessional becomes just one duty among others, but a particularly tedious one, and uncomfortable too. Confessions follow one another with monotonous regularity inducing a certain somnolence, so that he hears only imperfectly the details and gains the impression that they are all very much alike.

In no other connection is it so vital to wage war against routine. Christ died and rose once and for all, and his death and resurrection are contained in confession, which is itself enacted as a unique and definitive event. The sacrament is something whole and undivided, and each sinner who comes to it has a claim on it in its entirety; it is this that brings him into contact with the one event of the cross and so with redemption. When the priest bears this constantly in mind, he sees at once that he must never let confessions become a routine. That would be almost the same as becoming hardened to the cross of Christ; and then the cross would not be a unique event, but just one historical fact among others, which would amount, fundamentally, to unbelief. The life of each person would, then, no longer be what St. Paul meant by "filling up what is wanting to the sufferings of Christ", a sharing in them; for, with the death on the cross, everything would be finished, and so without meaning for us living now. Its whole meaning, in fact, would have been accomplished in the past, and we, redeemed once and for all, could, after each sin or any number of them, use the present as we please. With the loss of its sacramental power would go, also, the moral efficacy of confession, together with all the personal influence the Lord intended to accompany the sacramental power, likewise the priest's responsibility before God, the obligation of faith. Faith would become a kind of customary observance; no one would need to bestir himself about it unduly or to attend to it overmuch. Confession would be no more than a dialogue on the human plane with reference to a long past event, but not itself a Christian event participating in the unique event of Christ's cross. A ceremony of that kind would foster the grave misconception, for which the Catholic idea of confession is often reproached, that one may sin as much as one likes, since confession is always possible; for, if it is not an event in the Christian sense, it is no more than a sign, constantly available, pointing to an ever-present fact. This sign would then be held so efficacious that the way in which confession was made and heard would have no importance at all. The penitent would, in fact, play no real part, nothing at all would really happen. In heaven he would be held absolved; on earth he would continue to be a sinner.

This distorted conception of the sacrament, and the consequent misuse of it, is attributable, in part, to a routine manner of hearing confessions. If only the formal side is seen and stressed, even in instruction for confession, the real content is lost. Then the priest has no need to give himself personally, participating in the Son's self-giving before the Father, a personal involvement which the Son made an integral part of confession. But, in fact, each confession ought to be, for the confessor as well as the penitent, a real Christian achievement, in which each gives himself in the fullest possible degree. Just as, in his miracles, Christ felt power going out from him, the priest ought to put into the miracle of absolution and the whole process of confession, something of his own spiritual substance. We may recall what Our Lord said to his apostles when he sent them out on their mission, after the resurrection; how they would work signs and wonders. These would be mainly those contained in his words and, foremost, in his sacraments. We are accustomed, indeed, to look on the Eucharist as an outstanding miracle, the miracle of transsubstantiation. In comparison, that of confession only too easily pales, and then becomes, as it were, congealed within its official and ecclesiastical framework. Too often the priest stops short at this latter aspect, oblivious of its real content. He concerns himself mainly with what constitutes its validity, and loses the sense of the infinite ramifications of the sacramental power that derive from the cross.

Yet the whole office of confessor has arisen from the most exacting personal striving of God himself, and therefore rightly demands a corresponding effort on the part of the holder. The bare "legal" requirement is but a minimum, whereas he must aim at the fullest personal commitment throughout. First, in his preparation for hearing confessions, then in the way he recites the prayers, from the heart and not just with the lips; in the way, too, in which he listens to the penitent's account of his sins, conscious of how they add something to Christ's suffering on the cross. Then in the counsel he gives, for he must be attentive to the word of the Spirit in order to find the right way to reach the penitent; he can only provide real encouragement and strength, point the right direction, if he gives himself completely to the working of the Spirit. Then in the penance he prescribes, for he must have the will to share in the penance of all his penitents, and he must select the penance that is most appropriate to its purpose. Finally, in the absolution, in which he too participates, in his sense of the grace given, his own unworthiness to serve as its channel, his sense of the joy it brings. And though the whole process is repeated over and over again, each time he must come to it alert and attentive.

The Curé of Ars may be taken as a model for all priests. The routine confessor may object that it is not given to everyone to be a Curé of Ars; and, in so doing, he fails to see that the grace of confession is indivisible and, as such, is imparted, in its entirety, to every priest, who can, in consequence, become such as St. John Vianney was. For, in his case, the significant thing is not his charismatic gift of seeing things his penitents failed to reveal, and of knowing things before they happened, but rather the way he gave himself in confession. His sufferings in the night, his weakness, the burden of his life that he could scarcely support, and which, from time to time, he sought to elude, all this shows how he committed himself to his penitents, and whatever grace he was given he imparted at once to them. He made himself simply a channel that received only to give, accepted what befell him so as to transmit the fruits to others. And if his perception sometimes failed and he made mistakes, that had to be accepted. How often, too, may he have given the right advice which was either misunderstood or simply rejected!

The confessor's personal involvement in confession is not just a matter of feeling. It is based on the Lord and his sharing in all the concerns of men, joining in their festivities, mourning with them at the tomb of a friend, weeping over the obduracy of Jerusalem, rejoicing at the revelation to little ones. In all this he was fully man, yet never separated from the Father and never disparaging his own divine nature. The Father's will, his own decision to die for sinners, was his constant inspiration. This basic disposition was no obstacle to his sharing in everything human; on the contrary, it helped him to do so. If the confessor keeps this always in view, the motives for which he originally assumed the office will remain alive and active, as also his faith and love for God; it will determine his basic attitude, which will ensure that, whenever his office claims his participation he will be there to give it. Each time he hears a confession he will apply himself to it with all his heart, as standing in the place of Christ; he will try to hear the penitent as the Spirit hears him, and that will help him to speak in the Spirit when he comes to advise. Then it will be literally true that, in his counsel, in the absolution and the prayers, he speaks the words of the Spirit. There should be no kind of opposition between the official and the spiritual aspect, between his word and that of the Spirit; each confession will be for him a real contact with the penitent, the grace of the risen Lord, and with the Holy Spirit, and thereby an enrichment of his own being.

The incarnate Word had a direct vision of the Father, yet we can never say that, to him as man, this vision was something habitual. Each encounter of the Son on earth with the Father was as new as his eternal encounter with him in heaven, and so, for the priest, his encounter with the Son and the Spirit in confession must always be a new one. From this standpoint, then, it is not difficult for him to make his encounter with the penitent something ever new. God concerns himself in each confession individually. Men become habituated to anything with time, and possibly we would, in the end, accustom ourselves to God and his grace, were this not the eternal encounter of God with God, in which God is never habituated to God, but which is ever new. That assures us that no custom need harden us, that we need not fear the general law of habituation. Some states we experience fade and expire with the passage of time as, for example, that of infatuation as opposed to real love, which is able to conquer time. In love properly so-called, one loves someone as he is now, but also as he will be in fifty years' time and in eternity, and is prepared to surmount whatever disillusionment time may bring.

Christ remained, all his life, in the same basic disposition. In this respect, it made no difference to him whether he feasted in a publican's house or died in an agony of thirst on the cross, whether he prayed to be relieved of the chalice which he, none the less, always desired ardently to drink. In the same way, the confessor may hear a tragic confession one day, and the next be present at some festivity. If his disposition is like Christ's, this will involve no incompatibility. At the feast he will not be so affected by the confession as to find it intolerable to be among sinners enjoying themselves, guilty of all kinds of evil or about to be. But his present joy and sharing in that of others will somehow proceed from confession and lead back to it, in the same way as all that makes up the ordinary routine of his life must be incorporated in his habitual priestly disposition, where he is in contact with the Lord himself, who, as Son, is ever one with the Father in the Holy Spirit.

Every time a priest hears a confession he receives a grace which not only makes him a better confessor, but also strengthens his whole priestly activity. Wherever he happens to be, and whatever his sphere of action, he will always conduct himself as a priest, bringing men nearer to God. Some kind of influence will radiate from him that causes penitents to confess better, and draws to the confessional those who have stayed away. If no disparity is discernible between his function and his way of life, then the various contradictions in other men tend to be resolved, contradictions between their sins and their joys, their good will and their obduracy, between their secular life and the sudden presence among them of a priest, between their worldliness and the fact that there is a God. All that a priest does as such, his very existence as a priest, reacts favourably on each of his different functions and each circumstance of his life. Whether in his work or his recreation, he will always be conscious of his responsibility before God; his sense of obligation to God grows continuously. Just as Christ, in all circumstances, was ever the Son of God and redeemer of the world, and all his life was lived in view of confession, everything in it being brought thereby into a unified whole.

Nothing in the course of a confession is without significance for the confessor. What he must learn is to give each part of the confession its due weight. The actual hearing of the confession seems, at first sight, to be what varies most, since each person has his own way of confessing. Here there are two things to take into account; the attitude adopted and the facts disclosed, of which the former is of greater moment. From the facts related the priest must draw a general view of the penitent's life, which enables him to distinguish the more important from the less. The provisional distinction he makes as the confession proceeds may be corrected or even discarded according to what follows later. In this preliminary stage he will attend especially to things more familiar to him, to what he has learned before and experienced in other confessions. He may classify what is told him under different headings: grave sins, very grave sins, doubtful sins, imperfections, and, in this way, form a general picture. While he does this, he sees, for example, through the order adopted by the penitent, how the latter thinks of his own situation and the respective gravity of his sins; but, even so, the confessor has not yet grasped what lies behind it all, the basic disposition. For there is a long way from sin to confession; and, though the confessor has to know the sins, it is no less important for him to see why the sinner has come to confession. The reasons are not self-evident. From the manner in which the penitent confesses it should be possible to see how he regards the sacrament, whether he is drawn by a sense of urgency or routine, etc. There are other indications of his basic attitude: his choice of words, the explanations he may or may not give, his manner in the confessional.

The confessor has to take account both of the sins confessed and the person who confesses. They are not to be considered in isolation one from the other, and, in particular, the confessor must not allow his preoccupation with the sins to obscure his view of the penitent. Confession involves humility, which is itself a grace, and this grace must be utilized. It too has a subjective and an objective aspect. The priest hears confession in virtue of his office; at the same time, he is a man who has chosen the way of this office, and, to reach the man before him, he must not allow his human qualities to be absorbed by his office. In the institution founded by the Lord he must see what the Lord has laid up in its heart; in the judgment he must discern the underlying grace, in the authority the presence of love.

At the start of a confession, the confessor attends mainly to the objective aspect. The sins he is told are little different from other sins; they have all been heard before. Then suddenly he glimpses through the recital of sins something of the man himself, the unique individual person; and this may cause the confessor to revise his whole estimate. All that is necessary is a kind of overtone, or something so slight as to be hardly expressible in words, to elict this second view. Admittedly, there are plenty of people of whom it would be difficult to detect anything of their real personality, but the attempt must always be made, particularly as the priest himself is always in danger of succumbing to routine. Unless he makes this effort, the number of those he can really make contact with and help will steadily diminish. On the other hand, if he really strives after this, their number will grow continuously, and he will keep, not only himself, but his penitents, from lapsing into routine. Sometimes there comes a point where nothing more can be done, since the penitent is too hardened in his ways; but the confessor must always try to sense all that he can from what he hears, and that not through some kind of psychological technique, but through attuning himself to the Spirit and with a view to the advice he will give. Even in the way he hears the sins the priest must co-operate with the Spirit.

Each confession is an entity on its own, but not an isolated one, for it harks back to previous confessions and prepares those that are to follow. The confessor, therefore, must always bear in mind that what he hears is not a disconnected series of sins, but a cross-section of the penitent's life. It is, indeed, a summary of his present state, but represents a period more or less long, and, further, the grace of this confession should fertilize a whole period in the future. The matter of the confession should enable the priest to see where he has to sow the seed, what point to take hold of for the benefit of the individual penitent. The penitent is a man on the way to Christ and eternal life, and he should be given something that strengthens him in his journey.

Ordinarily in the life of the Christian there are few opportunities for the priest to intervene for the express purpose of moulding his life. Confession is one of the chief of these. In Communion he gives him the body of the Lord, but delivers over the communicant to its action; he himself can hardly intervene personally. If, however, a man became a priest in order to bring to the Lord as many souls as possible, he must always remember that, in that regard, the confessional is a privileged place. However rigid the general framework of confession, there is still wide scope for the human qualities of the priest, by which, a sinner himself, he can help other sinners. As a sinner, he is part of the community of sinners, but, as priest, he is in communion with the Holy Spirit, whom he must allow to work freely in him. This presupposes in the priest great docility and purity of intention, and also personal effort, for it is through his action that the Spirit works.

Insight into the penitent's whole disposition is important on two accounts; first, in order that the appropriate counsel be given, second, to enable the confessor to pray according to the penitent's needs. There is a kind of sacerdotal prayer that arises out of hearing confessions, and it presupposes that the priest correctly judges the state of his penitents. There is, of course, his general prayer for all penitents, whose beneficiaries are unknown to him; this resembles the Church's treasury of prayer. It should be supplemented by his prayer for definite individuals, which requires that he should know their needs.

The decision to become a priest implies the will both to serve the Lord and to help others to come to him. Service to man is twofold: to men in general, of whom the priest knows only indirectly, by general report, how deeply involved in sin they are, and to a particular group with whom he is in contact, whom he knows individually. While still a student, the future priest should envisage these as "his", and pray for them in particular. Every penitent is a representative of all sinners, but, at the same time, a particular individual with his own need of absolution. Both these aspects must be present to the priest, and this demands of him a constant alertness of mind, so that he perceives the individual as such, and also his involvement with the vast anonymous mass of mankind. Thus the penitent imposes on the confessor a twofold obligation, towards himself and towards all others. Everything here is both individual and general. The individual confessor is bound up with all other confessors, and among his penitents there may be future confessors, who learn from him what it means to confess and hear confessions rightly, and have a special claim on his prayer.

Often in conversation with people we have the feeling that there is something amiss, the situation is obscure. Someone describes some happening, and we accept what he says, though we know all the time it could not really have been like that. We ourselves may get involved in some misrepresentation, and cast about to get at the truth without being able to find it. There are, no doubt, excuses; it was time to break off, or we were too tired or ill. But perhaps the real reason was that we were not sufficiently on the alert.

Here the Curé of Ars can serve as a model. He was never surprised into this sort of situation. He took his stand in a truth far greater than his own, and remained there consistently. He did not separate his own truth from God's, but made it all part of the truth of the confessional. He told people the truth to their face, and the truth forged its own way into them. The situation he created was very often completely different from what the penitent wished to bring about. What he did was to make them participate in God's way of viewing the matter, and to place them, without their awareness, in a situation where they could see properly. It was not that they wanted deliberately to mislead him. They really desired to confess their sins; but they did not see them in the true light.

The Counsel

The confessor must always remember that he speaks in the name of the Holy Spirit, that he must allow due scope for the Spirit's action. The Spirit is God, and the confessor his representative. The words he speaks must be uttered reverently in the Spirit; he receives them from the Spirit, and must accept them in humility and as serving the Spirit. The form he gives them is his own, but the content is the Spirit's; and though he has to speak plainly and without affectation, it must yet be in a way that allows the Spirit his proper place. Through him the penitent must make contact with the Spirit.

The Son was fully human, and, despite his divine nature, retained all his human characteristics. The priest, too, in the confessional must keep his own personality. His words, while uttered in the Spirit, must also convey his own personal involvement, his knowledge, his designs. He must manifest the fact that he acts along with the Spirit, and not speak in a languid, indifferent manner. The sinner has to be brought into contact with God through his relationship with his confessor, as one man with another. Consequently, there is bound to be, on the part of the priest, some intervention in the intimate relationship of the individual with God; the penitent, by his confession, has given him a right to this. The priest, however, must intervene in this sphere only with the greatest reverence, since, at the moment, the penitent is in close contact with God. The priest is there present at a process which makes a sinner into a saint, and his words must serve to accompany this transformation, in fact, to lead the sinner into it; consequently, they must be so tender and yet so telling, so penetrating, that the change is effected simultaneously with their utterance. They should have the power to stir up in the penitent a disposition which will allow no impediment to the growth of sanctity. Absolution, of course, comes as a turning-point given from above, but it does not work like magic. The penitent has his part; he must make his way as if through a tunnel, along which his confessor goes with him, and at whose end absolution awaits him. That is a way which only God can carve out, but it can be traversed by man if accompanied by another who takes the place of God.

The counsel itself has a twofold aspect, according as it envisages the penitent both as one among the whole mass of sinners and also as this particular individual. The absolution too has these two aspects. Further, in the counsel given, it must be borne in mind that the penitent has undergone the humiliation of confessing his sins and so proclaimed his will to finish with them and to follow the way of God. As a particular individual he must be shown his own special way, and made to see it is possible; at the same time, as a sinner like all the rest, his way must be the universal Catholic way.

It is often best to frame the counsel so that its first part bears on the matter just confessed, brings out aspects unnoticed by the penitent, motives hidden from him, reasons for his lapses; but always in such a way that he can draw some practical conclusions. Moral exhortation is not enough; as far as possible, the penitent's situation must be related to the great truth that comes down from the Trinity, through Christ, to the Church and the individual, but this must be done so as to open up to him a new mode of life. At the same time, it is not just his personal way that has to be indicated, but how it fits in with the whole Catholic idea of life. He must become not merely a better man, but a better member of Christ and of the communion of saints. For that purpose, his understanding must be widened and deepened.

The counsel given by the confessor must be the outcome of his own life of prayer, and this should be perceptible by the penitent. In his confession the penitent has admitted the confessor to his close confidence; and now, in the counsel, though in a different fashion, he should be admitted to share the confidence of the confessor, in that he is given a certain insight into his life of prayer. It is only in the sphere of prayer that any intercourse between the Holy Spirit and the confessor is at all possible; and, within the sacrament, there comes into being, between confessor and penitent, a certain community of life which, though a matter of extreme discretion, is very close and intimate. The priest acts instrumentally, and this means, not that he conceals himself behind his office, but that he reveals himself in it, and gives away something of his inmost self, though this must never, in any circumstances, be made liable to abuse. It is an act of confidence and trust, a mutual one, though differently for each, since it requires, on the part of the penitent, a certain keenness of ear – itself a function of faith – to perceive it. It is not a thing that can be apprehended by the ordinary powers of the mind, but belongs to a sphere accessible only in prayer. The main thing to remember is that here the Spirit speaks and manifests himself; consequently, the confessor must not take himself as an example to give point to what he says, but remain always completely objective. When what the confessor says is of very special moment, it happens that, later, the penitent will hardly be able to recall the exact gist, but will remember how it sounded and where the way indicated ought to lead. In confession, the penitent's condition becomes such that he cannot hear the confessor's words otherwise than as spoken in the Holy Spirit.

For his counsel the confessor should make use of words that recall passages from the gospel. This will make the penitent feel himself brought back into the sphere of the Church and thereby into closer contact with the life of Christ. Certainly, the counsel should be practical and personal, but presented in such a way as to make the penitent feel the living presence of the Lord in his divine word. Just as in preaching it is fundamentally the gospel that must be proclaimed, so also the counsel, though it should not be a sermon itself, must yet teach the gospel.

It should finish with a concise summing-up, enabling the penitent to remember better what has been said and to impress on him what was meant for him personally.

Spiritual Direction

The counsel given by the confessor is, in essence, a form of what is known as spiritual direction, whose nature may now be elucidated. Each individual member of the Church is directed by her in the sacraments, which express and effect their own special kind of contact with the Lord. The Christian may be considered as an individual and as a member of the communion of saints, and, in both aspects, will be subject to the appropriate direction; in the latter, through the Church and the sacraments, including confession; as an individual, through his particular director and in special circumstances. These are present, when the confessor judges such direction to be necessary because he recognizes in the penitent a special calling, or when the penitent himself expresses the wish for such direction because he desires closer union with the Lord and does not know how to attain it. In the second case, the confessor must first be convinced of the necessity for special direction. If it is urgent, then there will be no difficulty for him to see it; the penitent, then, only asks for what God moves him to ask. Direction is almost always required when it is a question of adopting a consistent, regular life of prayer and contemplation. Then it is for the confessor to choose the required means. He may enter more closely into the penitent's confession, and make his counsel more detailed and particularized in prescribing certain rules for him; or else he may appoint another time to discuss the main question.

If it is the penitent who expresses the wish, the confessor should go closely into his reasons, seeking the aid of the Holy Ghost in the confessional. There may possibly be hidden motives of self-seeking, the penitent wishing to have more notice taken of him; or perhaps he is subject to some mental disorder and wants to use the priest as a kind of psychiatrist; or he may be drawn for a time to the idea of spiritual direction for reasons of snobbery, but have no intention of persevering. It is not always easy straightaway to see the real motives, but they should become clear after two or three sessions. If the penitent's desire is justified, then it rests with the confessor to determine whether he is to be directed in view of a more perfect spiritual life without any special mission or definite apostolate, to a more harmonious development of his life of faith, or whether, perhaps later on, a definite mission is to be envisaged; whether, in the beginning, everything in general is to be fostered and encouraged and a definite choice to be made later, or whether a particular way is to be prescribed immediately.

To guide a person on the right lines, the confessor must try to make the best possible use of confession. He will lead his penitent in virtue of a special light of grace arising from confession, going thoroughly into the means for enabling the penitent to overcome his failings, prescribe certain readings, spiritual exercises, meditations on Scripture. But the aim of direction is always positive; the soul is emptied of sin in order that the love of God may pervade it. To put the matter simply, we may say that the main function of the confessor is to set free from sin, that of the director to foster growth in divine love. Freedom from sin, the concern of the confessor, it something that can be verified, but positive progress cannot, consisting, as it does, in humility, childlikeness, which cannot be measured, in acceptance, too, of God's will. In any case, calculation must be quite ruled out. The penitent submits to the action of God; his own difficulties and successes, which before served to measure his advance, are now of less moment, only to be mentioned if the director expressly requires it. All his efforts now must be bent to stir up a hunger for God, to let the Son's own disposition work more strongly on and in his soul, to become more and more sensitive to what the following of Christ demands, to the inspirations of the Spirit. This presupposes that the penitent's life be all of a piece, his inner and outer life harmonious, his conduct towards his confessor in accord with that at home and at work. Spiritual direction is of no avail without complete honesty on the part of the penitent, and the confessor must be convinced this is present.

Spiritual direction is hampered by the fact that many, not to say most, penitents fail in complete and absolute openness, that unalloyed Christian disposition. The penitent ought to be wholly taken up into the Lord's own way of thinking, wholly penetrated by him; the more strongly entrenched he is in this, the more easy he finds it to renounce having any distinct view himself. The confessor, however, must always keep the whole situation in view, for it is just when the penitent cannot, and should not, see any more that he needs a director. Even if the direction may often be quite supple and contact with the director infrequent, it is still imperative. It is, therefore, for the director to decide when circumstances demand a more precise and detailed form of direction; and when he is convinced this is necessary, he should enter on it with the greatest tact. For if the penitent is too early apprised of the fact that he may have a special mission, or that everything is working towards it, he may either falter or be unduly elated, or possibly become anxious about pride creeping in. He has to be made aware that direction is necessary at the moment, without concluding that this implies any special distinction. It may seem a paradox, but it is absolutely true, that the more exceptional the penitent's way is, the more he must be made to feel that he is just one of the generality of mankind, for, in fact, the more unusual a person's mission, the wider its influence on the whole communion of saints. If the penitent sees that the confessor is directing him in a special manner, he should look on this as a kind of "consecration" of himself, yet without dwelling on the fact, and more with the sense of his inadequacy for the service required than of being specially singled out. It is as if he were told to sweep the floor, but someone has to take the broom from him and show him how to do it. He thought he was quite capable of the more skilled work, and now he needs someone to teach him even the elementary kind. Spiritual direction is a great school of humility.

It is one also for the confessor, who now no longer preaches "on the mount", but turns to instruct a handful of disciples. On him too the Lord screws up the pitch of his demands, giving him a more detailed insight than a priest usually obtains. He has to learn to adapt himself to a more stringent direction from the Lord, so as to make himself capable of directing others.

Prayers Used in the Sacrament

The prayers used in the administration of the sacrament place both priest and penitent in the framework of the Church: they are fixed and unalterable. In the order they follow they form a single whole, and effect what they signify; their meaning is what the Church intends and prescribes. On the one hand, they serve the purpose of a final safeguard for the effectiveness of the whole procedure, independently of the particular confessor and penitent; they are an expression of its authoritative nature. On the other hand, they are words of power and life expressing tender concern for the penitent, and inclining the confessor to do his utmost for him. They are a perfect expression of the reality of the situation, appropriate to every case, combining the two aspects of the sacrament, the official and the personal.

(May the Lord be in your heart):

Dominus sit in corde tuo that is, before the confession begins. The Lord must be in control; the sacrament is wholly his gift and property. There he acts in what is most specially his own domain. From the outset he must rule the heart and lips of the penitent – no disparity between heart and mouth – so that the confession of sins may be entire and as ordained. And though the sacrament belongs to the Lord, it is enacted in the name of the Father, the Son and the Holy Ghost. It is the Lord's gift and bears his warrant, but is carried out in the name of the Trinity, as is everything else effected and established by the incarnate Son on earth.

(May the almighty God have mercy on you):

Misereatur tui omnipotens Deus. This prayer, which follows the priest's words to the penitent initiating him into a new life, expresses the essence of the sacrament, that it is for God to have mercy. Confession, contrition, counsel have meaning only in view of this mercy on the part of God. It is no mere formula or just a wish, but a prayer of the Church for what she is bound in obedience to request and will unfailingly be granted her, that is for the absolution assured by the cross. As a prayer of the Church, it must be pronounced by the priest with the utmost attention and reverence. It is no formality, but the Church speaking with God. The priest's attitude must be not different from that of the Church, any more than it is in hearing the confession, in the counsel he gives, and in the prayers; they should all spring from one and the same prayerful disposition. The penitent himself has a right to this sacerdotal prayer.

The words of absolution derive their efficacy from the cross. Of the various scenes in the life of Christ some may, in time, come to play little part in the priest's meditations; he may, for instance, not feel drawn to that of the child in his mother's arms, his own childhood being so remote. But the scene in which Christ gave his apostles the power of absolution can never lose its force; it is constantly recalled in the confessional, as also, either directly or indirectly, in his commerce with men. It sums up the whole life of the Lord, comprises all the mysteries that directly concern him as priest; the more he thinks about it, the more he finds there. Every time he says the words of absolution, he feels himself newly endowed with the power coming to him down the centuries from the Lord himself. At that very moment he is contemporary with the Lord, with the cross and the resurrection. That is the moment of the sinner's encounter with the redeemer, and he, the confessor, is the one who mediates it, speaking the *ego te absolvo* with a sense of his utter unworthiness. Yet this does not deter him from the duty, at that moment, to pronounce these words. His unworthiness makes no difference, for he is appointed to speak them; they are the Lord's words and, therefore, they are the Lord himself.

Ego is a word that means the Lord and, at the same time, includes the priest. It points to the Lord's office while comprising that of the priest, but also the Lord's love including that of the priest. The priest, out of his love for Christ, chose this way of serving him; and it is in virtue of his priestly life that he can appropriate the fruits of Christ's life and impart it, as his own, to others. He shares in them, not in the manner of a servant remote from his master, but as a friend in close intimacy; and shares in such a degree that the Lord not only lives in him, but speaks the word *ego* in him, takes him up into his own being and action. The words of absolution are words of sheer miraculous efficacy, and which if they were to lose, in the slightest, their connection with the Lord, would be mere blasphemy and pretention. But because they are the Lord's words, they can lend themselves both to the Church's authority and the priest personally, without thereby ceasing to be his. They can be uttered in perfect simplicity, but a simplicity pregnant with mystery.

Ego *te* absolvo. The *Ego* absolves the Thou, who has just

confessed, and can now leave his sins behind him, because the Lord has satisfied for them. This Thou is present as something whole, yet as an isolated thing that seeks to be restored to the wholeness of the community, though itself coming forth from the wholeness of a community, that of the Lord and of the Church in the priest. In the *Dominus vobiscum – Et cum spiritu tuo* of the Mass, what is primarily addressed is the unity of the congregation, and the priest stands before it as an individual apart. In confession the repentant sinner is the individual, who stands before the community of the Lord and the Church, and through it is incorporated anew in the communion of saints. He will have no need to feel himself a stranger there; he will already be bearing the Lord's mark at this second coming, and so will be acknowleged as his. His temporary estrangement has not made him a kind of second-class member of the community; on the contrary, he returns to it newly enriched with the gifts of grace. In fact, he came to confess as a member of the community. Through his sin, he had isolated himself, but the Lord restores him to harmony with the community.

Ego te absolvo. It is the Lord of life and death who speaks, the Lord who brought Lazarus back from the company of the dead. Lazarus was absolved from his death; no one can now speak of him as dead, since he is now alive. Death is entirely wiped away, wholly supplanted by life, for no one can be both alive and dead. In the same way, the sins of this individual sinner are wiped away, in whom life has replaced death; and this, although at the time they were committed, when they were being repented of, they had such a tremendous reality, belonged so unmistakably to him who had done them.

When the Son was sent by the Father to be a man amongst men, he continued to possess his vision of the Father, yet what he took to himself, namely human nature, he took in its entirety.

He did not will merely to be man at certain moments, and between-whiles God. None the less, he always remained the incarnate God. Something of the same completeness he demands of those who desire to follow him, something of that he gives those who desire to follow him, something of that he gives those who abide in him. They are not to be half sinners and half saints, but wholly saints; nothing is to impair their belonging to him. He frees them from their sins not just partially, so that they have to drag them along behind like chains. He puts himself between sin and sinner to separate them, cuts the bond and changes the whole existing situation according to his good pleasure. Once a person has confessed, he should no longer see his past sins in any other light than that given by God, just as the Samaritan woman, freed by the Lord from her sins, knew, indeed, she was a sinner, but lived henceforth wholly in the grace just given.

In all that concerns faith and the life of faith what matters is not so much one's own personal approach and way of envisaging things as the way willed by God. Otherwise, if we were left to our own devices, our prayer, for instance, would very soon be wholly circumscribed by our own interests or come to be rather like drawing up a long list of requirements. But if we pray as God wills, our preoccupation with self grows less and less. It is the same with all that concerns faith. Once our sins are confessed, they lose all importance, and deserve to be remembered only in function of the grace given. If we confess rightly, as far as one can, we come to see something of this mystery of being freely led by the Lord, and subordinate the consciousness of our confessed sins to this guidance of his. We will, indeed, be aware of them in some degree, but should not desire to know them otherwise than as the Lord shows us them. It is for him to determine the extent and manner of their continuing effect, not for us to say what influence they will bear on our life in the future. A life of penance for past sins can, at best, serve to bring out the greatness of the affront done to God; but even so it must be seen objectively. One's own sins can be a starting-point and an occasion for this consideration, but nothing more. What is important now is not sin, but God alone, who loves us, whom we offended. Ultimately, indeed, it is not even a matter of who has offended him; for the life of penance is a part of the Church's life, which does penance for all that displeases God.

On all this the Lord gives enlightenment to each one. He may, perhaps, on occasion, desire us to look back on our past sins, institute a personal "contemplation of sin"; but this must proceed from obedience in faith. No one should think that the more he reflects in horror on his sins, the more worthy he becomes; in fact, it would be absurd to try to gain merit through contemplating one's own demerit. The contemplation of sin in the first week of St. Ignatius' Spiritual Exercises is itself performed out of obedience; both the duration and the subject matter are laid down. The important thing is not sin, but conversion, and that the exercitant be initiated into the new attitude he must have from the second week onwards. Admittedly, there is also the opposite danger, that the penitent should consider himself disassociated from those in sin. Contemplation of sin can also serve the purpose of implanting in us the Christian conviction that we are, indeed, sinners; but it must not be forgotten, either, that the whole sequence of exercises was intended to be a unique occurrence in the life of the Christian, and that the main purpose of the "first week" is to make one realize at last what confession really means.

Auctoritate ipsius (By his very authority). The authority of the Lord remains permanently with the priest for him to apply, in his official capacity, without having to renew it in each case. It is for him to decide whether to absolve or not. He has it in virtue of his office; but it is not the "power of the office", it is the power of the Lord.

Ab omni vinculo excommunicationis et interdicti (From every bond of excommunication and interdict). All that can possibly separate the penitent from the Church is removed. The Church enumerates these obstacles, and, when the penitent is a priest, adds the word *suspensionis*. The penitent is to return fully absolved and purified, newly bound to the communion of saints. *In quantum possum et tu indiges;* as far as the priest has received power from the Church to remit also ecclesiastical penalties, and as far as the penitent needs such remission. The precise nature of the terms rules out in advance any misapplication; for it is the Church that mediates the Lord's power to the individual priest, and, though its power of binding and loosing is complete, the priest cannot loose what the Church intends to bind and what it does not, at the moment, will to loose. An interdict may lie on a country or a town, and so on an individual who has no personal guilt and yet may die subject to it. The Lord will take him to himself, since his grace is not restricted by the plenitude of power belonging to the Church. It is possible too for someone to be excommunicated without being aware of it, and to be released while still in ignorance.

Passio Domini nostri Jesu Christi. . . . The Passion of Christ is the first thing to be mentioned after the absolution. We were the cause of the cross, and so we owe it to the cross that we are freed from our sins. Previously, in our preparation and confessing, we had to place ourselves before the cross as sinners, and now, freed from sin, we must enter in gladness with the cross on a new life. Along with the Passion mention is made of the Mother of God and of all the saints. Previously, we were alone with the Holy Spirit, there was no mention of any company;

we stood in isolation to be judged. Even when the priest prayed for us, helped us, we were alone. But now that we have been restored to the community, we can behold once more the saints of the Lord, whose merits are the fruit of his Passion.

Consequently, we are placed along with them under the law of the cross. The cross is not only what we were responsible for, not only the achievement of the Lord by himself alone, but also the community of all who live beneath its shadow. In that the fruit of the cross is imparted to us, we share in the communion of saints and so possess a claim to eternal life. Provided that we remain what absolution has made us, we are assured of eternal life.

Absolution restores the penitent to the company of all who stand beneath the cross, so that all that he does and suffers in the spirit of faith contributes to the salvation of all. Once more, he is a living member of the one Church in its active apostolate. Nothing in his former life that was of value to the Church is any longer to be considered void. All he did and suffered is meritorious, because incorporated, by grace, into the merits of Christ and his mother. And, from now on, such action and suffering is a debt he owes, an obligation laid on him by the priest, whose words he must continually bear in mind. A twofold obligation: to do what is good, and not to shrink from what is burdensome. Both of these were perfectly fulfilled by the Son, the apostolic work set him by the Father, and the apostolate of suffering prescribed likewise. Only the Passion of the Lord is explicitly mentioned, but his whole image must dominate the conduct of the penitent in each particular, both his acts and his sufferings. His acts necessarily involve acceptance of what befalls him; on both the Lord has a claim, because he himself performed both, and only the two in combination make up an integral Christian life. Action must not be allowed to encroach on acceptance, any more than the Lord himself could have allowed his sufferings to be outweighed and thwarted by an excess of good works. The words of absolution contain a warning against activism.

After Confession

The penitent takes up his ordinary life again, but in a new freedom and a new kind of obligation and with a wholly different emphasis. The external side may be unchanged, but the spirit informing and animating it is quite different. Previously, when he carried the burden of guilt, it affected, to some degree, his daily work; he and his work were not wholly in accord. Now that he is making a fresh start, he must purify his attitude to his work, however secular it be. No longer is there any reason to complain of the monotony and futility of life, no reaon for sadness and depression; he has in himself a new power enabling him to make his life an expression of the word of God. The very same things he used to do under compulsion he does now in freedom of spirit, following the Lord and sustained by his presence. His life is a continuous act of praise of Christ, real and not just simulated.

Admittedly, confession, more than the other sacraments, has a tendency to induce in us a feeling of hopeless resignation. We all know that, in spite of all we have promised, we are still subject to the temptations of the world. We have, indeed, been made free, but we do not really believe in our freedom, and so we abandon it before long to the enslavement of sin. We entertain within ourselves all sorts of objections, in fact, we stand in the way of our own progress. We do not really believe in the strength given us by the Lord in confession, and, if it is not to grow weak, it must be constantly exercised. Only if it is allowed to be active in our life will it remain vigorous.

The strength newly given derives from prayer and the Christian attitude implanted in us by the Lord. Externally, our life has nothing remarkable to show, nothing in the way of a radical change. Grace is something within us; it comes from the Lord and has to return to him. Its fruits belong to the Lord, so much so that they may always remain imperceptible to us, make no impression on our environment, least of all change our outward life. For if this were its result, it would be ascribable, in some degree, to our own efforts; we would look on ourselves as successful persons, vigorous and energetic. We would have harnessed the strength given in absolution to finite ends, rather than to those of eternity. Conversion is not something that can be proved by displaying its moral effects before the astonished eyes of our neighbours. Certainly, there ought to be some change, even in our surroundings, but it arises principally from prayer and the interior disposition, which can produce their own effect in the world. This change, however, is not the first object of our striving, but rather the service of the Lord, which pertains to eternity and is not something temporal and of immediate effect. How the world is changed by this service is mainly the concern of the Lord. We are defenders, not of our own interests, but of the Lord's.

As for the confessor himself, he may, when he has finished hearing a number of confessions, feel a certain discouragement. Perhaps among his penitents were some whom he knew well and whose state has deteriorated, others who seem always subject to the same failings, and yet others who seem not to have understood what he said to them or not to have taken it to heart. Many too only wanted to receive absolution and to go away as quickly as they could. In view of all this, the priest may tend to be sceptical about the value of the sacrament or of his own adequacy as a confessor. However understandable this feeling, he must not give way to it. What he does he does in the spirit of faith, and he must see to it that his faith and trust grow steadily the longer he goes on administering the sacrament.

His duty to his penitents does not end with absolution; he must continue to pray for them. He can console himself with the thought that it is not his own strength, but that of the Lord, he dispenses, whose apparent powerlessness is itself a form of strength. The priest is not to judge by results, but remember that, through his office, the Lord can help him far more than he suspects, and that it is his duty to his penitents to keep as close as possible to him. Priest and penitent, after confession is over, remain in contact by prayer, binding one another more closely into the communion of saints; and the penitent, through his prayer, brings new grace for the confessor for his subsequent confessions, both those of the penitent himself and of others.

The Power of Binding

In granting the power of retaining sins, the Lord shows the gravity of sin and what a serious matter confession is. The confessor uses the power given him by the Redeemer, and consequently must act according to the Spirit of God, and make his decisions, as far as possible, coincide with those of God; for it is a revealed truth that God also distinguishes between cases in his judgment.

The Redeemer indicates the possibility of sin being retained, but this does not mean a limitation of his love: it is, rather, all part of the act of love by which he instituted the sacrament. The retention of sins can and must be seen as an expression of his redeeming love just as much as is their forgiveness. Both have the same end, that of bringing men back to God's love. One whose sins are retained is not, for that reason, rejected, even though the way to absolution is made more difficult for him, for this is done precisely to increase his love, and to enable him, on his return to the communion of the Church, to bring a greater contribution of love that he can at the moment.

The confessor who has to withhold absolution must pay particular attention to the counsel he gives the penitent, who would not have come unless he had expected to be absolved. Presumably the penitent had underestimated the gravity of his condition, and is now in a more humiliating position than he was at the start of his confession. The aim of the confessor must be to give him strength and encouragement, to bring him to submit humbly, to prepare the way for absolution in the future; and the blessing the priest gives instead of absolution should be accompanied with fervent and insistent prayer for him.

The Secret of the Confessional

The institution of confession followed closely on the mysterious events of Holy Saturday, whose imprint the sacrament always bears. As far as Good Friday is concerned, we can always form some idea of what happened then, imagine to ourselves the cross and its physical torments, the thirst and the exhaustion that culminated in death. We can recall all the sufferings Christ endured, the humiliation and anguish, making them more and more vivid to our minds; at least we can think we can gain, in this way, some idea of what our redemption involved.

But nothing in our experience gives us any insight into the

mystery of Holy Saturday; our imagination wholly fails us here. It is a profound secret between the Son and the Father. What we know about it from revelation is so little, so oblique, that no one can imagine himself to have any definite idea. It is all enshrouded in silence, the silence of death, of the unfathomable abyss between death and the resurrection. It is a silence more eloquent than any speech, being the silence of the Father and Son in the closest intimacy; silence, none the less, because the Son, on his return from hell, said nothing about this mystery.

It was then that he instituted the sacrament of confession, into which enters something of the silence of this mystery, as the final seal on the work of the cross. In confession the priest takes cognizance of the penitent's sins, their number, kind and circumstances. At the same time, he perceives, through the attitude of the penitent, much of what is not directly disclosed as to how he stands in regard to the Father and to the Church, of his intercourse with God both in speech and in silence. He divines something of the inmost being of this penitent, something perhaps of which he himself is unaware and which lies outside the range of direct perception. All this he apprehends only in the context of the penitent's confession of his sins, not independently of it, like the Son on Holy Saturday. That is the reason why the priest, since he learns more of the sinner in confession from his silence than from what he says, has himself an obligation of silence. There are many other reasons, more obvious, but they are only subsidiary to this. The penitent must be certain of being protected from any possible indiscretion or misuse. It is in order to be absolved by God that he confesses to God, and God has appointed a man so that the confession of sins may be a more human procedure, more true and conformable to Christ. The confessor is the embodiment, in visible form, of Christ and of the Church, for the benefit of the penitent, and so the intimacy between the latter and God remains unimpaired.

When the priest dismisses the penitent, he consigns him to the deeper silence of God, in a sense to the mystery of Holy Saturday, where the Son gained the grace of redemption in its most profound and mysterious elements. So it is that the priest is obliged to the most absolute silence by regard for the mystery of the Son and therein for the penitent who had the courage to confess, for his attitude before God.

What the priest knows from confession can furnish him with matter for prayer. It is his to use to make his ministry more fruitful, not to gratify his curiosity. He has no need to strive either to forget or to remember what he has been told, but should simply accept the state in which God places him. For spiritual direction, certainly, he must remember the more important things, using them to bring the penitent nearer to God and the Church; others he can well forget. Often it may be useful and necessary to ask the penitent's permission to speak about his previous confessions in order to discharge his responsibilities as a confessor. He may need to know about previous sins, whether the penitent has forgotten their recurrence, or sees them otherwise than before, no longer taking them seriously, or whether they have really been conquered. Here it makes all the difference whether he is dealing with someone who comes to him only occasionally or is habitually directed by him.

11. THE CONFESSION OF SAINTS

THE CROSS is where holiness is to be found, the supreme holiness of which the Son of God, in dying, gave a last evident proof. On it is the God who put aside his majesty, making it over to the Father: on it the man whom God has made holy in each particular of his life. All holiness springs from there, even that of the unsullied, the innocent, who, were this possible, may have borne no share of the cross. All holiness comes from the cross and goes there, not, however, to the empty cross, but to the crucified Lord, who there gathers up in himself his entire life on earth and, indeed, all that makes up the Church's holiness, her life of faith.

Confession is the fruit of the cross; and at the very moment when this fruit is put at the disposal of the Lord, he hands it on to others. In making his ordinance about confession, the Lord makes it plain that this fruit is now in his possession, at the same time as he imparts it. We can contemplate this fruit in confession, just as we can perceive his flesh, himself, in the consecrated host, with this difference, however, that we contemplate it in confession, not as something subsisting there, but as something to be performed. Visible as it was in the moment of being imparted, for us it is apprehensible only in the execution of the act. And each of the saints confesses as a member of the community of all believers, in order to obtain a share in this fruit, and not so much to obtain absolution for his own sins as to come to the place where the fruit of the cross is given visible form. He confesses, in fact, so as to make it more visible still, to be a partaker of it and even to share its engendering on the cross, to make, through his own confession, the Lord's word of grace once more incarnate in the mystery of holiness he ordained. His confession is linked in a close bond with the sacrament of communion; it is itself a eucharistic act.

The saint gives confession a certain distinct quality, and he alone can give it, one so precious that we might almost think that the Lord had it specially in mind at the institution. It is precisely the saint, the man who has sinned least, who can pronounce the perfect confession, that of his estrangement from God. It is also a confession that includes all sinners. The saint's confession is, more than any other, a social, ecclesial act, one in which all sinners participate.

We can distinguish three classes of saints: those who were sinners and know by experience what sin is; those who have never sinned and do not know sin from experience: those who have not sinned, yet know what sin is. They can be represented, accordingly, by St. Francis, St. Teresa of Lisieux, and St. Aloysius.

Francis had once been a sinner. Now he sees his sins not only separately, but as a whole aggregate of offences to God. His love for God burns within him, burns ever more ardently, so that it consumes his whole being. And the truer and deeper his love, the truer and deeper becomes his sense of the outrages continually added to by sins, not only his own, but all other sins that come to his knowledge. When he hears that this or that evil has been done, or that others today commit the same sins as he used to, in the same state of part-knowledge and part-ignorance, when he sees that sin takes priority over love, then it is that he confesses. His confession then is, as it were, the focal point of all the accumulated offences against the Lord, a point that burns more fiercely the more his love increases. As love consumes him, he feels ever more strongly how much more consuming it ought to be, and along with this goes an intensification of his sense of the outrage to God. Sin, then, in his eyes, falls into various categories which he recognizes through the sins he himself committed; and what he confesses is, in one way or other, the fact of estrangement from God, as does every saint in this group. For example, though he no longer practises deceit, yet he has not loved truth enough. He no longer injures others, but he has long not given them all that he could, all that real love would demand. Thus what he confesses is like a reflected image of his own sins. Now that he sees better the outrage to God, his former sins show him the shortcomings of his present virtues. He sees this, not in a theoretical kind of way, but as a present, pressing reality. What he has become, he sees, is someone who has merely replaced his former sins with a state of tepidity, who, despite his clearer knowledge, fails to respond to the urgent demands of love. It is, then, as if he were confessing over and over again his former sins, which appear in an ever fresh light, the more conscious he becomes of his responsibility. For, just because he does not deceive any more, he ought to have a burning love for truth. And every confession sharpens his perceptions, intensifies his feeling of unworthiness, yet, by no means, drives him to despair, for he is conscious of grace. The greater his sense of unworthiness, the more certain he feels that God's mercy extends even to a sinner like me!

Teresa of Lisieux had her own particular form of confessing, which corresponded to her own special knowledge of sin.

Fundamentally, it was never really clear to her what sin was. She had a kind of intimation that people did things that were offensive to God, and that these had particular names, such as lying, theft, murder, hatred, pride, self-love. But these things and their names had no essential relationship to herself. For her, evil was the contrary of good, but this was a rather vague and abstract relation. Sin and everything to do with it was something frightening; she thought and spoke of sin rather like people do of things they would prefer to keep silent about. This attitude of hers is clearly reflected in how she bore herself in regard to what is called her "night". Her sufferings brought her as far as the mount of Olivet, knowing and bearing, as she did, the sins of others. But, in fact, no one can really know precisely what the agony of Olivet is, if he does not clearly envisage the cross of Golgotha; and so with Teresa it was always something like a groping round about sin. On "Olivet" one cannot fully measure the extent to which sin is an outrage to God. In her confession, therefore, Teresa accuses herself of small, even trifling, matters, but never manages to reach the standpoint of Francis in his. She is overjoyed at never having committed a mortal sin, but this awareness restricts the scope of her confession. She never gets beyond the stage of preparation, as Olivet was a preparation for the cross. She tries to go forward, advances at times, but never gets to the end. There is even a tinge of exculpation in her confession, but she is always ready to bear more, and glad to be in the community of penitents. In this context, the stress so repeatedly laid on "littleness" can, occasionally, bring about a certain diminishment. Both her confession and her knowledge of sin fall short of complete insight, clarity of vision, realism. But in this group of saints there can also be found cases of perfect confession, when, that is, the saint lets himself be led right up to the cross, not by anticipating the Lord's stripping action in him, but by an attitude of abandonment which, when the moment comes, is not just a passive self-oblivion, but an active acceptance of what is then disclosed. For even those who have never sinned must learn to know sin. It is really part of Christian courage not to be content with less than clear vision, and to know that, after "Olivet", however painful it be, there comes the real cross.

St. Aloysius is quite different; he is more like St. Catharine of Siena. Sin makes him suffer, and he does not evade the pain. He is capable of looking on sin firmly and objectively. Though he has no part in it, has never felt the chains of sin, he knows it. He has the will to know what it is. When he feels it unbearable, he at once thinks of how it was unbearable to the Lord. Nor is it his endeavour to establish just how he stands, how far he is involved and how far not. His past enters little into his calculations. He is thankful to be able to do what God expects of him at the moment. Had he committed a grave sin, it would be something shocking indeed, but he would confess it and then go on forward. But if he knew that he had never sinned, he would very likely have thanked God for it, without dwelling on it unduly. He also confesses his estrangement from God, but without searching closely into its cause. He keeps his gaze firmly on the superabundance of God's grace, and confesses that wherein he falls short. And all this not just on the theoretical plane; in this he closely resembles St. Francis. Nor does he theologize about the sins he sees others commit. He sees them as believers like himself, his brothers even, who do not love enough; but still nor does he love enough. And so, though he is capable of distinguishing specifically their various sins, he feels himself at one with them in their lack of love. He considers it inessential whether it is their want of love that caused these determinate sins, or, as in his case, prevents love being more ardent. His contrition has its source in his knowledge of how he falls short of the demands of love. Consequently, we cannot say that, for him and those like him, there is not "matter" for contrition, and so no absolution. He has a strong sense of the grace of absolution, stronger than St. Teresa, and this gives his love a new impetus.

The Mother of God cannot feel excluded from the community of penitents, because she shared, in the highest degree possible, the penitential attitude of her Son. She shares in the confession of all sinners, inasmuch as the Son, as man, is perfectly open before the Father, his openness as God being imparted to his humanity. Mary sees this absolute openness of his, and, though perfect herself, strives unceasingly after it, unattainable though it be. She strives without looking to the result. For her the essence of the penitential attitude is this: resemblance to the Son. There is no absolution as far as she is concerned, instead the closest proximity to the Son as Redeemer and purifier of all sinners.

Also from Herder and Herder

THE PRAYER OF ALL THINGS

PIERRE CHARLES

The subjects of these meditations are the ordinary things of everyday life. They are so much part of our common experience that we tend to disregard their spiritual significance. Yet God has evidently made them as proofs of his revelation and glory. They are aspects of the incarnation of the divine Word. By reflecting on them we can be led to their Creator. It is because man is a material being that his salvation, in the Christian view, should be in and through this world. However, an old error persists to this day, which induces many of us to separate "the things" of the spirit and "the things" of the world. Consequently we tend to regard the world of ideas as noble and great and the world of things as common and despicable. The result is that prayer, spirituality, the approach to God sometimes become intellectualized, wearisome abstractions of human realities.

It is to combat this false approach that the late Pierre Charles, an eminent and popular Belgian priest, wrote this book. He has selected texts from the Gospels which sing the praise of God's animate and inanimate Creation. Each of these "things" — shoes, roads, clouds, trees, doves — has a spiritual lesson to teach; that is why they are mentioned in the Gospels, and why, by fixing his attention on them, the reader may be helped to raise his mind and heart to the Creator. The author is incidentally concerned with combating various forms of religious escapism, such as denouncing our own times and exalting the past or dreaming of some remote future. With all the simplicity of a great spiritual writer he shows man's salvation to be here and now.

Also from Herder and Herder

PRAYING WITH CHRIST

HEINZ SCHÜRMANN

It is the author's aim to elucidate the Lord's Prayer from his message and, conversely, to discover in it the key for that message.
This treatment of the Lord's Prayer is based entirely upon the Scriptures. The relevant words and acts of Christ are grouped in the form of summarized sections, each of which opens up vistas into the whole of the Christian message. This is done in a very simple manner, without scholarly apparatus, although the book is a definite work of scholarship. However, the author is not concerned with abstract theology but with conveying the living message of the Lord: "We must plunge into a new world which is communion with Jesus. There we shall learn that we may understand his word in the measure in which we are able to say his Prayer, and that we shall learn to say his Prayer in his spirit in the measure in which we listen to his Word."
This elucidation of the Our Father is thus "devout" in a real and theological sense. Man in his existence is confronted with God. He has to face him in all seriousness; he has to give himself to him. The tension of being a Christian is vividly shown in God's kingship which both is and is not yet. The author begins with the two traditional forms of the Our Father, which he compares literally. These result in the two main divisions, the prayer for the coming of the Kingdom of God and the three petitions as three necessary concerns of the apostles in the expectation of this Kingdom.
The reader is shown what is meant and what he asks for when he says the "Our Father", and what is asked for by these prayers. This is living and practical theology with an appeal both for the expert and the layman, providing both with a new approach to the Lord's Prayer, in which sound knowledge and edification go hand in hand.

Also from Herder and Herder

TIMES OF GRACE

The sign of 40 in the Bible

ROGER POELMANN

Introduction by John L. McKenzie SJ

It is common knowledge that the biblical revival has had a marked impact on the progress of the liturgical and ecumenical movements, on dogmatic, moral, and ascetical theology, and on the entire aggiornamento of modern Catholic thought. It is equally well known that this influence has only rarely been reflected in the devotional literature of the ordinary Christian, with the result that much popular Catholic piety remains outside the mainstream of the Church's life in the twentieth century.

Times of grace is a volume of spiritual readings which aims at opening up to *all* Catholics the new and important insights which have been disclosed by modern biblical scholarship. This, then, is not a work of scientific exegesis, but a meditative treatment of the scriptural theme of "forty days". The number of days or years denominated by this figure was a sacred period representing a cycle of preparation and attainment, of penance and redemption. The Christian of today, who during Lent imitates Christ's forty days in the desert, will come to realize through this book that those forty days were the fulfillment of all preceding periods of forty in the Old Testament: of the forty days and forty nights of the flood, of the forty days of Moses on Sinai, and of the forty years that the chosen people spent in the desert before entering the promised land. In his Lenten renewal of the spirit of the "forty days" the modern Christian thus will recognize his own place in that history of salvation which extends from the Fall to the present day, and on into the future.